Hinsdale Public Library - Founded 1892

A Gift To The Library From

Joyce & Lee Person

In Memory

Helen Hench Jones

Hinsdale Public Library
Hinsdale, Illinois 60521

BAKER & TAYLOR

Gardens of the Heartland

Gardens of the Heartland

Laura C. Martin

PHOTOGRAPHS BY Allen Rokach

Abbeville Press ❧ Publishers ❧ New York ❧ London ❧ Paris

For Bill Brenner — To the Heartland and Beyond

COVER, FRONT: *The Bur Oak Garden at Cantigny, near Chicago, offers spectacular displays of color during the growing season.*

COVER, BACK: *At Kingwood Center in Mansfield, Ohio, the gardens are a splendid place to visit in all seasons, especially the fall, as shown here.*

FRONTISPIECE: *Brilliant shades of fall leaves create a colorful backdrop for the formal, clipped boxwood hedges at Kingwood Center, an estate in Mansfield, Ohio.*

PAGES 4–5: *Mist rising from the lake envelops trees and a bridge which connects a tiny island to the main part of The Dawes Arboretum in Newark, Ohio.*

EDITOR: Susan Costello
DESIGNER: Celia Fuller
PRODUCTION EDITOR: Abigail Asher
PRODUCTION MANAGER: Lou Bilka
LINE ILLUSTRATIONS: Bobbi Angell
TYPESETTER: Barbara Sturman

First edition
10 9 8 7 6 5 4 3 2 1

Library of Congress Cataloging-in-Publication Data
Martin, Laura C.
    Gardens of the heartland / Laura C. Martin ; photography by
Allen Rokach.
        p.   cm.
    Includes index.
    ISBN 1-55859-781-6
    1. Gardens—Middle West. 2. Botanical gardens—Middle West.
3. Arboretums—Middle West. I. Rokach, Allen. II. Title.
SB466.U65M535   1996
712'.0977—DC20   95-37434

Contents

Appendices

Preface

IN EXPLORING THE gardens of the American Midwest, you will find places that are historically rich, educationally exciting, and visually stunning. Each garden discussed in this volume is a world unto itself, worthy of visiting time and again.

The goal for most of these gardens is to present landscapes pleasing to the eye; to this end, millions of annuals, perennials, trees, and shrubs have been planted for the simple reason that they are beautiful to look at. Not all of the gardens included in this volume have expansive displays of flowers, however. Some, such as Old World Wisconsin and the Shaker Village of Pleasant Hill, were included because they represent an important part of the development of gardens in the Midwest.

The people from the midwestern states have created many exciting gardens for myriad reasons: as a tribute to the lovely natural landscapes once found in the region, because the splendor of the garden during the relatively short growing season makes up for the long, cold winters, or just because creating a place of fragrance and beauty is such an innately important thing for so many people.

The Midwest has often been called the "breadbasket" of America because of the miraculous productivity of the soil. It could also very well be called the "garden basket," for this same rich, black soil has made possible some of the most memorable landscapes in America. Gardens of the Heartland is a tribute to the many people who are determined that the heartland of America will remain a region of beauty.

"Everywhere in America there are two pictures, the vanished past beneath the living present." So said Walter Havighurst, in his book The Heartland. Nowhere is this more true than in the public gardens of America's Midwest. In these celebrated places, the past has taken root and grown and blossomed into the gardens of today.

Water Willow
(Justica americana).

Introduction

A History of Midwestern Gardens

THEY CAME FROM *places far and near, the settlers of the Midwest, drawn by the stories of endless prairie, inspired by the idea of rich, black earth. They came for land so fertile it soon became known as "America's breadbasket," and they came for the open spaces so vast that the prairie seemed to touch the sky at the horizon. Once Daniel Boone penetrated the wilderness and found the lush bluegrass country of Kentucky, settlers came in droves down the rivers and the Wilderness Road. For many, though, the lure of the West was strong and they continued their journey.*

Although the midwestern region of the United States is composed of many different kinds of ecosystems, from the great North Woods to the floodplains of the Mississippi River, it was the prairie in its startling expansiveness that caught the attention and imagination of the early settlers.

"The scenery of the prairie is striking, and never fails to cause an exclamation of surprise," wrote J. Plumbe, Jr., in 1839. "The extent of the prospect is exhilarating. The verdure and the flowers are beautiful, the absence of shade, and consequent appearance of light, produce a gaiety which animate the beholder."

This exhilarating prairie, stretching for hundreds of miles, covering acre after numberless acre, was the jewel of the American Midwest. This grassland was so stunning that the European immigrants who came here wrote and talked of it incessantly. To some, it was the most beautiful landscape they had ever seen; to others, the vast open land was frightening and intimidating. To all, the prairie was an experience never to be forgotten.

Some found the solitude overwhelming. Washington Irving, who traveled through the prairies in the late 1830s, wrote, "To one unaccustomed to it, there is something inexpressibly lonely in the solitude of the prairie." Jens Jensen, noted landscape architect from Chicago and advocate of the "Prairie Style," wrote of the landscape in a different vein:

Tiers of red-speckled Asiatic lilies (Lilium sp.) *bloom at Dow Gardens in Midland, Michigan.*

I watched the miles and miles of flat Nebraska prairie come into view. My fellow passengers expressed themselves as being bored with the monotony of these vast plains which had neither a tree nor an elevation to break their bleakness. There seemed to be an 'unending nothingness' as one passenger expressed it. But as I sat watching, I gradually began to feel a great force arise from these flat lands, and I knew that here lay something far deeper, far more powerful, than anything I had experienced before in the great out doors.

Pioneers said the grass was so tall you could tie it together over the back of a horse. But tall grasses were not the only plants in this flat wilderness. Here, also, were wildflowers of every hue, like the purple spires of gayfeathers, pink asters, and white wild indigo. Here too was the huge compass flower, whose stems, covered with large yellow flowers, sometimes grew ten feet tall.

Willa Cather, in My Antonía, *wrote: "As I looked about me I felt that the grass was the country, as the water is the sea. The red of the grass made all the great prairie the colour of wine-stains, or of certain seaweeds when they are first washed up. And there was so much motion in it; the whole country seemed, somehow, to be running."*

During spring and early summer, bogs, lakes, and marshes commonly covered large areas of this rich land, and the new blades of grass appeared emerald-green in the gentle sunshine. As summer heat matured the grass, it began to change colors until autumn found the prairie golden-brown.

It was not all unbroken grassland, however, as trees created punctuation marks of dark, rich color, particularly along creek banks. Chief among the tree species braving the sunny prairie was the bur oak. More oaks than other types of trees were found in prairies, perhaps because oaks could better withstand the raging fires, both man-made and natural, that were a natural part of the prairie ecosystem. Fire helped keep trees out of the prairies; grasses burn quickly and are not harmed by the same fires that kill the sprouts and seedlings of trees and shrubs.

Raging fires, harsh winters, swarms of mosquitoes in summer, and year-round solitude proved too much for many folk. It was only those to whom the prairie spoke who stayed to find joy and peace in this vast new land.

Even those who stayed found life on the prairie a frustrating and difficult experience. The soil underneath the tallgrass prairie is rich and black and reaches down twelve feet, the result of the decomposition of thousands of years worth of grasses and roots. Unlocking this fertile ground proved to be a monumental task, for the sod formed by the prairie grasses is tight and seemingly unbreakable. It was said that it took five yokes of oxen to break the soil, and the term "sodbusters" was soon a popular nickname for those people who stayed to farm the prairie lands.

Today, tragically, the prairies that originally covered so much of the Midwest have gone the way of many native ecosystems. Only small patches of this once-vast grassland remain. Today efforts by conservationists, horticulturists, and botanists have resulted in many successful restoration projects, making it possible to see a vast expanse of the prairie as it once looked.

Not all of the Midwest was formerly covered by prairie. Lakes small and great and the largest river system on the continent also had tremendous influence on the development of the land.

The rich bottomlands along the Mississippi River have attracted people for many centuries. It was here, between 900 and 1200 A.D. close to present-day St. Louis, that the Cahokia Indians built the most elaborate and sophisticated city north of the Rio Grande. Boasting buildings equivalent to modern ten-story structures, a population of more than 30,000 and streets and docks, this civilization dominated trade, manufacturing of tools and jewelry, and large-scale corn farming. The remains of this civilization can be seen at the Cahokia Mounds Historic Site, where a visitor's center houses excellent interpretive displays.

Centuries later and many miles to the north, a different group carved a civilization out of the wilderness. Hundreds of European settlers and pioneers headed west to find a new home in a new land.

The lure of the West seemed irresistible, and during the first few decades of the nineteenth century, people came in droves, not only from the settled regions of America, but also from Europe, particularly from Ireland and Wales, Germany, Scandinavia, and the Slavic countries. For those who traveled westward to the great North Woods, the scenery was quite different from that of the prairies. It was a deep, rich forest full of towering evergreens. With the opening of the Erie Canal, the trip west became much easier, and in the 1830s, steamships on the Great Lakes were a common sight.

By 1840 the midwestern frontier had essentially been settled. In 1836 J. M. Peck, who wrote the New Guide for Emigrants to the West, said, "Such an extent of forest was never before cleared—such a vast field of prairie was never before subdued and cultivated by the hand of man in the same short period of time. Cities and towns and villages and counties and states never before rushed into existence and made such giant strides, as upon this field."

And so the towns and cities were built and the prairies and forests were subdued, but were never forgotten, for the heart and spirit of the midwesterner still remains close to the land. Today the people of this region have paid tribute to the past and homage to the future by holding firm to their roots and creating public parks and gardens that evoke the natural wonders of the past, imitate, emulate and even perhaps improve on the present-day natural landscape of their region.

The same rich, black earth that made the Midwest the envy of the agricultural world today provides fertile ground for the growth of many kinds of gardens from the utilitarian herb gardens at New Harmony to the magical children's garden at Michigan State University. The harvest we reap from these gardens is an experience of awe and wonder at the successful union of plants and people—the garden.

Botanical Gardens

IN 1925 THE noted botanist Liberty Hyde Bailey addressed the Ohio Botanic Garden Society and spoke about botanical gardens in America:

A botanic garden is one of the agencies for the diffusion of knowledge of the vegetable community, although its significance is little understood or appreciated amongst us. The botanic garden is of early origin, but it has not yet been applied to any extent to the needs of modern life because the establishments are so few. As its possibilities are understood, the botanic garden will come to be an essential form of public expression and service . . .

How fortunate for us that Dr. Bailey's words have proven to be so true. The idea of a botanical garden as an institute to serve the public took root in the minds and spirits of Americans, resulting in a wonderful proliferation of public gardens that stretches from coast to coast. It is in the Midwest, however, that several of the first botanical gardens in the country were founded. Among these, the Missouri Botanical Garden, founded in 1859, and the W. J. Beal Botanic Garden, begun in 1877, are the two oldest.

These two gardens were begun for very different reasons. Beal Botanic Garden was started by W. J. Beal, a professor at Michigan State University. His original idea was to plant trees, shrubs, and flowers as a living laboratory for his students. He had few funds and began by moving a few wild plants from neighboring fields, woods, and bogs. He admitted that if he had waited until he had enough money to build a botanical garden, it probably would never have been built.

Henry Shaw, on the other hand, had sufficient funds to begin his garden in a big way. Having spent several years traveling in Europe, Shaw was very familiar with European architecture and landscape design. It was his dream to create a large garden for the people of St. Louis.

The idea of creating gardens and landscaped areas for the enjoyment of the public was certainly not a new one, but it was not until the end of the nineteenth century, when the civic beautification movement gained momentum, that the idea took firm hold on the American imagination. Influenced by the grand European gardens open to the public, and conscious of the need for such resources in our own country, people of wealth and influence began to look toward creating gardens for the people, particularly in urban areas.

The 1893 World's Columbian Exposition in Chicago (celebrating the 400th anniversary of Columbus's voyage) resulted in the creation of the City Beautiful Movement, the first organized effort at urban beautification. At the Exposition, horticulture was presented as an art form distinctly different from agriculture. Frederick Law Olmsted, in conjunction with the Exposition, designed 190 acres of interconnecting waterways and naturalistic plantings for the city of Chicago.

The Columbian Exposition itself was in many ways a precursor of the modern American botanical garden. Olmsted's grand park design for Chicago allowed visitors a glimpse of urban beautification, and other exhibits at the Exposition sparked interest in public garden displays. For example, it was here that the first Japanese garden in America was exhibited.

The beautiful displays and exhibits shown at the Exposition fired the imagination of many city leaders, and beautification became a civic cause worth fighting for. Daniel Burnham, in reference to Chicago's City Beautiful Movement, said in 1909, "Make no little plans. They have no magic . . . let your watchword be 'order' and your beacon 'beauty.'"

Many factors combined to help the beautification movement grow into the establishment of parks and gardens throughout the country. The 1930s brought economic depression but also brought such programs as the Civilian Conservation Corps and the Works Progress Administration, providing the manpower to build such beautiful gardens as Boerner Botanical Garden in Milwaukee, Wisconsin.

The botanical gardens in the Midwest today carry with them the original goal of serving the public. To this end, these institutions emphasize education and conservation along with their beautiful displays.

H. T. Darlington, who served as director of the Beal Botanic Garden after Dr. Beal, once said that "the best way for a botanic garden to grow is to grow naturally, adding new features which seem to give promise of real value. A progressive botanic garden is always dynamic, never static."

During the past few decades, botanic gardens have kept this in mind as they have expanded and grown in size and philosophy. Even as early as 1925, Dr. Liberty Hyde Bailey said, "Without active effort at local conservation we shall soon loose [sic?] much of the charm of the wild and free places, with the growth of population and the propagation of indifference to native surroundings." Since that time, many botanical gardens have made "active effort" at both local and worldwide conservation part of their mission by conducting research in developing landscape plants that can withstand difficult environmental conditions, and offering support and manpower for research in tropical botany. To better meet the needs of all citizens, many of these institutions have built gardens for the physically impaired and include programs in horticultural therapy in their educational offerings. For schoolchildren without resources to travel to a botanical garden, outreach programs have been developed where teachers and "plant mobiles" go to local schools to talk to the children about botany, horticulture, and natural science.

Janet Poor, in her acceptance speech for the 1994 Garden Club of America Medal of Honor, said, "Our botanical institutions must collaborate with teachers and schools to ensure that a child understands the world of nature and his need to be a part of preserving it. Equally important is the continued preservation of worthy plants—to sustain our biological diversity, to contribute to our need for medical properties, to enrich our horticultural palatte [sic?]."

Botanical gardens today offer places of beauty and education to their communities, where people can learn about what to plant in their own home gardens, attend formal lectures, and receive more in-depth information about a variety of botanically oriented subjects. But perhaps more importantly, people can come to botanical gardens to sit and dream. Although physically, many of these gardens are located close to metropolitan areas, philosophically, they are worlds away from the stress and pressures of city life.

People from all over the world have visited the botanical gardens of the Midwest, and most might agree with Francis Bacon, who wrote in his essay "Of Gardens," "God Almighty first planted a garden; and, indeed, it is the purest of human pleasures; it is the greatest refreshment to the spirits of man."

Missouri Botanical Garden

St. Louis, Missouri

WHEN THE 1875 *Compton's Pictorial* said that "the Missouri Botanical Garden is the finest floral garden in the United States," no one disputed the claim. Shaw's Garden, as the Missouri Botanical Garden has always been affectionately nicknamed, was one of the earliest and remains one of the most magnificent and important public gardens in this country.

Henry Shaw, founder of the Garden, came to the United States in May 1819. He was only eighteen years old when he moved to St. Louis, bringing with him a stock of cutlery from his native Sheffield, England. He hoped to find a ready market in this busy town on the edge of the frontier.

Of his first glimpse of St. Louis he wrote, "In passing, the town had a cheerful appearance, some of the houses being elegantly built with wide verandas, in the Louisiana style . . . There were no buildings on the river, but on the top of the bank were gardens, with fruit trees in bloom, forming a pleasant prospect . . ."

The "pleasant prospect" of these gardens made an indelible impression on the young entrepreneur, and decades later he was responsible for creating gardens of great beauty and promise.

Henry Shaw had enormous success with his cutlery line and by 1823 had increased his business to include items such as sheet steel, English razors,

Three pools, all built in 1913, reflect the image of the Climatron, a geodesic dome that has become the trademark of the Missouri Botanical Garden.

Originally known as Mr. Shaw's Garden, the Missouri Botanical Garden opened in June 1859. The development of its world-renowned water lily collection helped draw tens of thousands of visitors in the early years of the garden.

buckles, wrenches, spurs, and household hardware. Shaw seemed to find life in the United States much to his liking, although he commented in a letter of May 1820 that the West was "a country of knavery, oppression, and slavery."

In spite of this, Shaw was soon trading English hardware for western goods such as furs, deer and buffalo hides, lead, and cotton, and he was realizing even greater profits. At the age of forty, Shaw decided that the fortune he had amassed was enough for any one man and quietly announced his retirement. Although he no longer spent his days as a merchant, Shaw continued to work his investments wisely and became increasingly active in real estate dealings in St. Louis. The unprecedented growth of St. Louis during the 1840s made these investments quite lucrative.

During this period Shaw traveled extensively in Europe. Although he was well educated in mathematics, the classical languages, and the arts, he felt that travel was educational, and the years he spent in Europe were important to him. Among the sights he saw, the gardens made perhaps the biggest impression. Especially influential were the gardens of Chatsworth in Devonshire, England, which inspired him to create a public garden of his own in St. Louis.

Before beginning his extended European trips, Shaw had purchased 760 acres of land, and it was the thought of this land and the garden he would build here that lured Shaw back home. By 1855 Henry Shaw had definite plans and dreams of the public garden he would build on the estate he called Tower Grove. This land had once been known as La Prairie de la Barrier a Denoyer, after Louis Denoyer, who tended the gate to the village of St. Louis. According to French-Canadian custom, land such as this was deeded to the heads of families in St. Louis, and was to be used for cultivating crops. Shaw had other ideas.

Probably because of his European travels, Shaw was well versed in both architecture and landscape design and had a clear idea of how he wanted to develop both Tower Grove, his country estate, and his home in the city. He hired George I. Barnett, an architect from New York. The working relationship

Botanical Gardens

18

The Linnaean House, named for Carolus Linnaeus, was built in the 1880s and is the only greenhouse remaining from the early days of the garden.

OPPOSITE. Henry Shaw's legendary attention to detail echoes throughout the garden. Here a miniature knot garden is intricately woven with flowers and herbs.

between Barnett and Shaw was a happy one and lasted from 1849 until Shaw's death in 1889.

To help him develop the public gardens he had in mind, in 1856 Shaw hired Dr. George Engelmann, a German-born physician who also had a great interest in and knowledge of botany. Engelmann sought the advice of Asa Gray from Harvard and Sir William Jackson Hooker from Kew Gardens in England, and the plans for a great public garden moved a step closer to becoming a reality.

Henry Shaw turned his considerable energy and business experience toward the garden project. He immediately went to work commissioning workers to erect a wall around three sides of a ten-acre garden area, design a museum and library, create a rosarium and erect plant houses and an entrance lodge. An opening in the wall was later made into an entrance gate, called Flora Gate.

His attention to detail was legendary, and in 1857 he wrote, "The Garden has been trenched over

two feet deep (cost $1,000.00) and in fine order for planting anything . . . I intend to have everything substantial and elegant . . . I shall commence the ornamental plantings next spring."

The gardens were designed in a formal European style. Parterred gardens were placed between the Tower Grove House, located on the south side, and a plant house northwest of the main gate.

When the museum building was finished, the Missouri Botanical Garden was opened to the public in June 1859. Although it was immediately popular with visitors, Shaw didn't seem satisfied and nearly ten years later wrote,

"The Garden was visited by increased numbers the past summer. I think not less than 40 to 50 thousand. I do wish we had something more interesting and instructive for the inspection of such multitudes."

In 1868 Shaw built the "Old Conservatory" and hired James Gurney, formerly of the Royal Botanic Garden in Regent's Park, London. Gurney originally had charge of both the formal gardens and greenhouses as well as the 285-acre park surrounding the Tower Grove House. Among Gurney's greatest contributions to the Missouri Botanical Garden was the founding of the water-lily collection, which eventually became known throughout the world.

Shaw's interest in science never waned, and in the early 1880s he erected a greenhouse dedicated to Carolus Linnaeus, the Swedish scientist considered the father of modern botanical nomenclature. The Linnaean House, as it was named, is the only greenhouse that remains from Shaw's time.

Henry Shaw died in 1889 and left almost all his property to a board of trustees, which was charged with administering the garden. (Careful about details, Henry Shaw not only had his own mausoleum designed, he even posed for sculptor Ferdinand von Miller to etch his figure in white marble to be used at the mausoleum.) Before his death, he requested that Dr. William Trelease of the University of Wisconsin be named chairman of the School of Botany at Washington University in St. Louis.

Soon after Shaw died, the trustees elected Dr. Trelease as the garden's first director. The task facing Trelease was daunting. Shaw's country home was in a state of disrepair, the walls were crumbling, and the old greenhouses were outdated and in need of renovation.

But even more important than the physical work was the responsibility Trelease faced in fulfilling Henry Shaw's legacy. In his will, Shaw mandated that the garden should be open to the public and "forever kept up and maintained for the cultivation and propagation of plants, flowers, fruit and forest trees; . . . and a museum and library connected therewith, and devoted to the same, and to the science of botany, horticulture and allied objects . . ."

In 1890, just a year after Trelease was named director of the garden, he submitted a Garden Report to the trustees, an act that has been continued every year since that time. The following year he published a paper on willow herbs, setting a standard of scientific excellence for the Botanical Garden that has been continued to this day.

The early 1890s were exciting years for the young Botanical Garden. At Shaw's request, his townhouse was moved from Seventh and Locust and was rebuilt on the grounds of the garden. The gift of the herbarium of the late Dr. George Engelmann and the valuable and extensive set of books of Dr. E. Lewis Sturtevant was the beginning of a botanical library that was to become one of the finest in the world.

The turn of the century proved to be a difficult time for the Garden. A tornado took out hundreds of trees, hail smashed 1,100 square feet of glass in the greenhouses, fire destroyed much of a plant house in 1902, and financial difficulties forced the trustees to sell some of the less productive areas of the Shaw estate. By 1904, however, the Garden was thriving once again, and an estimated 300,000 people visited the Garden while in St. Louis for the World's Fair.

In 1913 John Noyes, destined to be one of the country's leading landscape architects, joined the Garden staff and made many important changes. In 1984 Barbara Lawton described the impact of Noyes's changes:

> Now one could stand on the steps of Tower Grove House and look north through the mausoleum grounds, across the Knolls and all the way to the Linnean [*sic?*] House. This eye line, by tying together two of Shaw's original constructions, brought a new larger cohesiveness to the overall design.

Through the years the Garden continued to grow, always on the leading edge of the horticultural world both in terms of floral displays and botanical research. One of the most stunning additions was the geodesic dome greenhouse called the Climatron, built in the early 1960s under the directorship of Frits Went. The Climatron was named one of the

Herbs—plants of medicine, magic, and beauty—intermingle with colorful ornamental flowers.

most significant buildings of the twentieth century by the American Institute of Architects. Today the Climatron houses the Garden's collection of tropical plants and continues to delight visitors.

The current director, Peter Raven, was appointed in 1971 and has brought the Missouri Botanical Garden to the forefront of the world's public gardens. Understanding that displays, education, and research are all of equal importance, Dr. Raven has strengthened the Garden's contributions in each of these areas.

Visitors sometimes feel overwhelmed at the prospect of trying to see all of the magnificent landscaped areas of the Missouri Botanical Garden. A trip around the garden by tram allows for a condensed tour. Visitors can then go back and explore at their leisure the areas of greatest interest.

The Ridgway Center is not only a visitor's center, but is also home to flower shows, an education greenhouse, and classrooms. A gift shop and restaurant are also found here. Just outside the Ridgway Center, a magical world of flowers and fragrance, fountains and statues awaits the visitors.

Springtime brings clouds of pastel blossoms to the Rhododendron and Azalea Garden just past the tram shelter. A path originating at the fountain plaza in front of the Ridgway Center winds through this area to the Rock Garden and Dwarf Conifer Garden. Low-growing evergreen shrubs are accented with bulbs, annuals, perennials, and native wildflowers.

The Shoenberg Temperate House, located behind the Rock Garden, replaced a Mediterranean House built in 1913 and taken down in 1988. Now, in addition to plants native to the Mediterranean region, visitors can also see plants from all temperate regions of the world including Africa, Australia, South America, China, Korea, Japan, coastal California, and the southeastern United States.

Next to the Temperate House, the geodesic dome of the Climatron is filled with exotic tropical plants from around the world. The dome is seventy feet high at the center, and spreads 175 feet in diameter at the base. Inside, pools, waterfalls, and lush green plants give one the feel of being in a tropical rain forest. This feeling continues when visitors step outside the Climatron and see the large pool in front of the building filled with gigantic water-lily pads.

Three reflecting pools built in 1913, holding collections of water lilies, extend from the Spink Pavilion (originally known as Flora Gate) to the Climatron. Seven works by the late Swedish sculptor Carl Milles were installed in this area in 1988. "Three Angel Musicians" perch on top of tall granite columns and seem to be keeping watch over all of the garden. The long pool by the Spink Pavilion is home to Milles's "Sun Glitter" and two "Orpheus Fountain Figures."

Between these pools and the Linnaean House, several small beds focus on individual kinds of flowers or flower types. In this area are a rose garden, bulb garden, hosta garden, and the scented garden.

The Linnaean House, built in 1882, is the oldest continually operating display greenhouse in the United States. The traditional gardens that surround it reflect the old-fashioned character of the building.

South of the Linnaean house is the Mausoleum, reached by a path that travels through the iris and the daylily collections. The Mausoleum, Museum, Lehmann building, and Tower Grove House are

RIGHT. *A stone lantern is found at the Japanese Garden called* Seiwa-En, *which means "garden of pure, clear harmony and peace."*

OPPOSITE. *The largest garden of its type in the United States, this Japanese Garden was designed in 1977 by Professor Koichi Kawana.*

In harmony with the Japanese idea of form and beauty, this lone pine tree has been pruned through the years to lend an air of antiquity to the garden.

clustered together. Just outside the house, a traditional herb garden holds plants used for culinary and medicinal purposes and a maze, patterned after the one Shaw planted in the 1800s, delights visitors of all ages.

The John S. Lehmann Building is home to the herbarium and library and is the center for the Garden's botanical research program, considered the largest such program in the world. The herbarium, a collection of pressed and dried plants, contains four and a half million specimens, including some collected by Charles Darwin in 1837 and on Captain James Cook's first voyage in 1768. Although the library is not open to the public, it is used extensively by graduate students and scholars from colleges and universities around the world.

Paths from the Lehmann building lead to the Rose Garden and the English Woodland Garden, where bulbs and flowers native to both England and the United States carpet the forest floor.

In 1977 Professor Koichi Kawana designed the fourteen-acre Japanese garden. This garden is called "*Seiwa-En,*" which means "garden of pure, clear harmony and peace," and it is the largest traditional Japanese garden in North America. The garden has a four-and-one-half-acre lake, and at the center is Paradise Island, composed of three large stones. Other lake islands are called Tortoise and Crane, both symbols of longevity in Japanese mythology. The innermost island, called Teahouse Island, contains a traditional teahouse surrounded by gardens; designed to be viewed from a distance, this island is not open to the public. Large Japanese koi fish live in the lakes and lagoons surrounding the islands and are favorites of children who visit the garden.

In almost all Japanese gardens, primary interest comes from the evergreen plantings, strategically placed stones, and carefully raked sand. In Seiwa-En, color also plays an important part. In spring the azaleas, rhododendrons, cherry trees, and peonies all have colorful blossoms. There are lotus blooms in summer and chrysanthemums in fall.

Always eager for new ways to educate the public, the Missouri Botanical Garden opened a demonstration vegetable garden in 1982. This garden displays vegetables easily grown in home gardens from spring until frost. An expansion of this idea is the Kemper Center for Home Gardening. In 1991 the first phase of the center opened; it included a pavilion containing a plant doctor, classrooms, displays, and a library. Scheduled to open in 1996, an eight-acre area dedicated to residential landscaping will include twenty-three different demonstration gardens.

The Missouri Botanical Garden offers instruction not only at the Garden itself, but also at other areas through an outreach program. Both children and adults, professionals and casual gardeners benefit from these programs.

The Missouri Botanical Garden is conscientious about upholding Henry Shaw's legacy of excellence, but the staff is probably most proud of the Garden's environmental research and plans for the future. At a time when the very future of tropical rain forests is in question, the Missouri Botanical Garden has taken an aggressive lead in botanical research. Under Peter Raven's dynamic direction, garden researchers, supported by a variety of government agencies and foundations, are participating in botanical research throughout the world, with special emphasis on the tropics. Today a total of fifty-five Ph.D.s are on staff at the Garden. These dedicated scientists work everywhere, from Missouri to South America and Africa, and conduct research that could be essential to saving many of the earth's plant species.

When he was seventy years old, Shaw described how the land he eventually developed into the public garden had looked when he bought it:

Subtle shades of red and green color a quiet pool reflecting the Japanese love of simplicity in a garden.

Botanical Gardens

. . . open to the river, a beautiful prairie extended westward, uncultivated, without trees or fences, but covered with tall luxurient [*sic?*] grass, undulated by the gentle breezes of spring, not a tuft of which can now be found . . . For a distance of two miles . . . no trees were growing; all was prairie, the long grass of which was annually burnt; it had for many years been left uncultivated, and had reverted to the state of a natural prairie, as it had probably existed from all times.

Henry Shaw had no way of realizing how important his garden would one day be, for the needs of the nineteenth century are distinctly different from those of the twentieth. As the Missouri Botanical Garden enters the twenty-first century, it is reassuring to know that the staff and volunteers who are responsible for carrying forth the dream at Shaw's Garden will continue to meet each new challenge with the same combination of determination and enthusiasm that has served the public so well.

Chicago Botanic Garden

Glencoe, Illinois

THE FOUNDING FATHERS of the city of Chicago were people of foresight and vision. They saw in their city, carved from endless prairie, not only a place for industry, but also a place of beauty. In 1837, Chicago adopted as its motto *Urbs in Horto,* "City in a Garden."

The idea of helping Chicago become a city of beauty was enthusiastically endorsed by leaders such as Dr. John Kennicott, editor of *The Prairie Farmer.* In 1853 he urged officials to purchase 300 acres of woodland just outside the city for the purpose of creating a city park and garden. Ironically, over a century later it was precisely this number of acres that was obtained for the creation of the Chicago Botanic Garden.

In 1871 the Great Chicago Fire destroyed much of the city, and any thoughts of developing parks and gardens had to be set aside. The fire left 2,000 acres of burned rubble; 250 people had been killed and 18,000 left homeless. In spite of these tremendous losses, the spirit of the people of Chicago was not dampened; a year later the city had rebuilt and expanded.

In the years after the fire, civic spirit was at a high point, and the Chicago Horticultural Society was formed in 1890. The purpose of this society was to bring together seedsmen, florists, and horticulturists to plan for the World's Columbian Exposition to be held in Chicago in 1893.

Horticulture Hall, built for the Exposition, was a magical place, boasting a huge crystal dome overflowing with flowers and plants. In addition to working at the Exposition grounds, members of the Society were also given the task of planting gardens and naturalized areas along waterways throughout the city. Frederick Law Olmsted was instrumental in designing these plantings, many of which can still be seen on Chicago's south side today. In writing of the Exposition, John Moses in his 1895 *History of Chicago* said it was a "green oasis in the arid desert of business and dissipation for the refreshment of the City's soul and body."

After the success of the Exposition, the Horticultural Society was not disbanded but continued to work to host flower shows and lectures for the

Carefully raked dry sand beds flank the path to the arched bridge that connects an island to the main part of this 14-acre Japanese garden.

community. The society's constitution, written in 1897, stated that "the object for which it is formed is the encouragement and promotion of the practice of Horticulture in all its branches and the fostering of an increased love of it among the people."

The Horticultural Society was successful in meeting these objectives until the end of World War I, when interest waned; by 1937 leaders allowed the charter to lapse. With the coming of the second World War and the National Victory Garden Program, interest in gardening once more boomed, however, and by 1942 it is estimated that 100,000 families were raising vegetables in the Chicago area. The Society was once again reinstated, this time as the Chicago Horticultural Society and Garden Institute, and volunteers were solicited to "make Chicago a better city and spread the gospel of good gardening."

The Society found a temporary home called the Garden Center just inside the Randolph Street entrance to the Chicago Public Library. In 1951 a small group of women, including chairman of the Garden Center Edith Farwell, began offering horticultural programs to the Chicago community. These women eventually formed the nucleus of the Women's Board, which has played a crucial role in the development of the Chicago Botanic Garden since the very beginning.

A written history of the Women's Board suggests that "the first requirement for membership on the Women's Board is a strong back." In addition to many strong backs, these women also offered innovative ideas and untiring energy.

For many years the Horticultural Society worked with the Forest Preserve District of Cook County, looking for a site for a permanent botanic garden. Finally in 1963 legislation was passed enabling the Chicago Horticultural Society leadership to lease 300 acres in northern Cook County for this purpose.

John O. Simonds of Pittsburgh was commissioned to design the gardens. His creative plans were based on the Garden of Perfect Brightness, built in 1709 in Beijing. Original plans called for the garden

to be composed of sixty acres of water and nine large islands. Although much of this early plan has been improved upon and refined during the years, Simonds's original concept of hillocks and waterways has remained, resulting in one of the country's most beautiful botanical gardens.

The ground-breaking, held on September 25, 1965, was the beginning of an exciting, and sometimes frustrating, time for the new garden. As Dr. Francis de Vos, first director of the Botanic Garden, described his first impression of the site, "My first look at the site for the Botanic Garden came on a cold, windy day in April. The first mound along the Edens Expressway was in place and a large sign indicating that a botanic garden was under construction was ready for background planting. The wind and sticky, impermeable clay were warnings that we were facing a long and difficult task, and that patience would be our greatest virtue."

His vision proved to be correct. Most public gardens in the United States have been established from existing private estates, but the Chicago Botanic Garden was planted from the ground up. It is the result of moving earth and diverting water to create a series of lagoons and islands. (The water not only adds a feeling of peace and beauty, but also moderates unseasonably cold temperatures, thus lessening possible damage to the plants.)

The Education Center, built in 1976, was designed by Edward Larrabee Barnes, who wrote, "It is uncommon for a garden to have such a water feature as this. When visitors cross onto the main island, they surely feel that they have left the everyday world . . . We wanted to keep cars away as much as possible, and that visitors should walk to the Education Center. This is very important when you are working so closely with nature."

A visit to the Chicago Botanic Garden begins with a drive through Turnbull Woods, a natural woodland area first acquired by the Forest Preserve District of Cook County in 1917. Peter Reinberg, then president of the Forest Preserve District of Cook County, said of this land, "In rugged natural beauty and splendid growth of timber no woodland equals the Turnbull tract . . ."

Today this area holds an outstanding collection of species indigenous to the immediate Chicago area. Early spring brings sweeps of soft colors from ephemerals such as bloodroot, toothwort, and trout lily. As the season continues, trillium and wild geranium carpet the forest floor. A nature trail through the woods provides the visitor with a close view of these spring beauties. The garden is composed of a main island and several smaller islands.

After parking in the lots located closest to the entrance, the visitor walks through the Gateway Center, across a bridge to one of the most exciting garden areas, the Heritage Garden. This garden was patterned after early European botanic gardens,

Petals of a lotus blossom (Nelumbo sp.) *fall open one by one.*

Soft lamb's ear, spiky thistle, and big globes of ornamental onion help to create a variety of textures in this planting at the Chicago Botanic Garden.

where a collection of plants was grown and studied for their potential medicinal value. Like most early botanical gardens, the Heritage Garden is divided into four quadrants. A statue of Linnaeus, father of modern botany, rises gracefully from one quadrant, reaching out a hand to welcome visitors to the garden.

The Heritage Garden is an outdoor classroom, a beautiful place to learn about the history of plants. Two of the quadrants display plants that illustrate in living color the science of taxonomy. Each of these beds is planted according to family and showcases

plant species with distinguishing characteristics. Key identification features are described on interpretive signs so visitors can differentiate one botanical family from another. Plants in the fourth quadrant are grouped according to the continent to which they are indigenous, effectively showing the amazing diversity of plant life found on the earth.

A rose is a rose is a rose, and Chicago loves roses. The Rose Garden, located at the east portico of the Education building, covers three acres and includes over 5,000 individual plants. It is one of the most popular areas at the Garden.

Trellises covered with climbing roses, soft green lawn areas, a fountain in the shape of an open flower, and a pool all add to the beauty of the Rose Garden. The roses are grouped according to color, with the farthest corners of the garden brought to light by the palest petal shades.

Follow the paths through the garden, past the fountain, and down the hill to the Waterfall Garden, where water cascades down a rocky formation into a quiet pool below. Although the waterfall is only forty-five feet high, careful plantings make it appear much higher. The Waterfall Garden is particularly stunning in fall, when maples and sumac blaze into color.

From the top of the waterfall, it is possible to see Sansho-En, "garden of three islands." This Japanese garden, an oasis of peace and stillness, was completed in 1982.

Sansho-En should first be observed from across the lake; this view will give the visitor a feeling for the garden in its entirety before individual components are discovered and savored. At the end of the arched cypress-wood bridge that connects the islands to the main island there is a large willow tree. Most of the garden, in true Japanese style, is characterized by stone and greenery with few floral plantings. Koichi Kawana, who designed this garden, said, "Simplicity must not be confused with plainness . . . Simplicity means the achievement of maximum effect with minimum means."

The effects of this garden are truly spectacular. A dry garden is raked to represent water, while close by, a moss garden colors the earth a delightful green. A *shoin* building frames a picture-perfect view of the lake and the gardens beyond.

Within the Japanese garden is a tiny island called Horaijima, the "garden of everlasting happiness." No bridge leads to this garden, for according to tradition it is reserved for immortals.

Back across the arched bridge on the main island, the dwarf conifer collection spills down the hillside, showing every imaginable shade of green. From dark green cedars to steely blue spruce, this garden is a unique collection of dwarf conifers, and demonstrates wonderfully the beauties of these plants for homeowners who desire to plant small evergreen trees and shrubs in their own gardens.

Just past the conifer collection is one of the newer gardens, the English Walled Garden. Planned by the noted English landscape designer John Brookes, this is actually a group of garden rooms, each representing a different style.

The Vista Garden is patterned after Christopher Lloyd's garden in Kent, England, and contains an octagonal pool. The view overlooking the lagoon and lawns is spectacular. The Pergola Garden is found at the northeast end of the Walled Garden. White and purple wisteria bloom abundantly here, turning the pergola into a riot of color and fragrance.

The focal point of the shady Courtyard Garden is a lead cistern dating from 1716. Plants displayed here show homeowners which species grow well in a shady formal setting. The Formal Garden is a tribute to the genius of the English landscape architect Gertrude Jekyll, and combines informal plantings within formal geometric beds.

The Checkerboard Garden earns its name from alternating squares of boxwood and silver artemisia. The Allee Wall Garden, featuring borders of flowering

Botanical Gardens

shrubs and perennials, the English Oak lawn, and Cottage Garden complete the garden rooms within the Walled Garden complex. A long, lovely perennial walk runs the length of the front of the garden.

The Landscape Garden, Naturalistic Garden, and Sensory Garden are also found on this main island area. The Sensory Garden places special emphasis on particularly fragrant plants or those with an unusual or interesting texture. Extra wide paths allow easy access for people in wheelchairs.

Visitors from all over the greater Chicago area come to the Home Landscape Demonstration Gardens for ideas on what to plant in their own back-yard gardens. Within this area are the Herb Garden, perennial beds, and the Rock Garden. The Naturalistic Garden is of particular interest to homeowners as it displays innovative ways of using increasingly popular native plants. Both woodland wildflowers and prairie species are grown here in appropriate settings.

A hop, skip, and jump over yet another bridge brings one to the Fruit and Vegetable Garden, where visitors can see the diversity of foods that can be grown in a home garden in the Chicago area. Old favorites and new varieties stand side by side, grown by tried and true techniques as well as new methods in the never-ending search for the best way to garden.

A geranium-filled pot sits on a stone wall at the Vista Garden. From here the visitor has a spectacular view of the lagoons and lawns of the Chicago Botanic Garden.

The English Walled Garden designed by British landscape architect John Brookes consists of a series of garden rooms, each representing a different style.

On a different scale, two other garden areas are dedicated to research. The Herbaceous Trial Gardens and the Plant Evaluation Garden are both monitored carefully throughout the growing season to determine which plants and which new cultivars grow best in this region. Results are important not only to the homeowner but also to nursery professionals.

With such an emphasis on water, it is not surprising that the Chicago Botanic Garden has an excellent Aquatic Garden. Close to the fruit and vegetable displays, water lilies and other aquatic plants can be viewed from a boardwalk built over the lagoon.

In spring, the Bulb Garden reminds us that patience is rewarded and that, in time, every winter turns into spring. There are over 250 species and cultivars in the Bulb Garden, including such favorites as narcissi, lilies, tulips, alliums, crocuses, snowdrops, anemones, and scillas.

To help the growing number of people who wish to participate in horticultural therapy programs, the Learning Garden was built for people with disabilities. Raised beds, vertical wall gardens, and wide paths make this garden accessible to many people who care for it lovingly. To dig deep into the earth and allow the soil to slip between your fingers is more healing than many medicines.

Many years ago Arthur L. Janura, general superintendent of the Forest Preserve District of Cook County, said, "You really had to be a dreamer to imagine what the Botanic Garden would ultimately become."

How wonderful it is that Chicago is full of people who shared the dream of creating a botanical garden, a place where people could come and enjoy some of the most beautiful flowers nature has to offer. Based on its short but glorious past, the Chicago Botanic Garden has a bright future ahead.

ABOVE. *The wide expanse of water, here with lotus blossoms in the foreground, at the Chicago Botanic Garden not only creates a beautiful, peaceful setting but also helps moderate unseasonably cold temperatures.*

ABOVE LEFT. *The Home Demonstration Garden offers visitors countless ideas and endless inspiration for planting in their own yards and gardens.*

Boerner Botanical Gardens*

near Milwaukee, Wisconsin

IF YOUR IDEA of a county park is an oak tree and a couple of swing sets, Boerner Botanical Gardens will change your point of view forever. A thousand-acre arboretum and formal gardens are not only a fabulous resource for the residents of Milwaukee County, but are also an attraction for visitors from all over the world.

In the early 1920s a young man who worked for the Milwaukee County Park System believed that parks for the people should include large, natural areas. Some people thought Charles B. Whitnall was a visionary with uncommon foresight and ideals; others thought he was simply a crank, because in the 1920s few people understood the need for wide open spaces and for a park where people could come and enjoy the out-of-doors.

Whitnall's overriding passion was a belief in the need for large rural parks that would improve the quality of life for people in cities. He once wrote, "City dwellers are like waterfowl trapped on a dusty prairie, restless and unhappy. It is the planner's job to lure them away from the modern, consumptive blight."

As a planner for county parks, he took his job very seriously and worked tirelessly until the County Board and Park Commission finally agreed that perhaps large rural parks would be advantageous to the community. The result was a parkway system that included over eighty-five miles of rivers and streams, and thousands of acres set aside for parks within the county.

Whitnall's dream was to create parks large enough to provide recreation, education, and inspiration for visitors, and to leave much of the acreage in a natural state.

"Animal and vegetation are complementary to each other," he wrote. "Nature requires an equilibrium, which is our object in maintaining sufficient park areas. Our welfare is dependent largely on living in harmony with the many laws of Nature— environment determines quality."

The first one hundred acres, originally known as Hales Corners Park, were purchased in 1928. A year later another 500 acres were added, and during the next few years more land was bought; the park finally totaled 660 acres in 1932. At this point the name was changed to Whitnall Park. Between 1934 and 1940, Whitnall Park and the Root River Parkway were combined, resulting in a total area of 3,266 acres.

Although the natural landscape was stunningly beautiful in this large, protected area, other visionaries held even greater plans for the park. Alfred L. Boerner, landscape architect for the county, believed that the park should offer not only natural areas but formal gardens as well. As a member of a family whose passion was horticulture (his brother Gene was a professional rose breeder), Boerner set out to make his dream come true by creating a formal botanical garden on the grounds of Whitnall Park.

He designed the formal landscape to look like a European estate garden and took full advantage of the dramatic views of the countryside afforded by the extensive land holdings of the Park.

In reference to the buildings found on the Park property, Boerner said, "Beauty is paramount in all park construction work because the one function of the park is to provide recreation for people in an environment of beauty. If a structure in a park cannot be built to be beautiful, it had better not be built at all."

In keeping with these ideas, the Garden House was built to resemble a farmhouse from the Cedarburg,

Wisconsin area. The building, designed by the local architect George Spinti, has hand-hewn oak beams and a beautiful carved mantel. The formal gardens were created around this building.

The physical labor needed to landscape the park and to create the gardens and the buildings was supplied by various governmental work programs such as the Civilian Conservation Corps, the Works Projects Administration, and the National Youth Administration. The majority of the work was done between 1932 and 1941.

Alfred Boerner's philosophy was that each park visitor should be provided with the opportunity for recreation and enjoyment, whether this included experiencing a formal garden, walking the trails of a natural area, or participating in more vigorous physical activities. To this end, parts of the park were developed into a golf course and picnic areas, while the remainder was left in a natural state.

A large part of Boerner's mission was in developing Whitnall Park to be a place of learning, and the most popular educational facilities at the Park proved to be the beautiful formal gardens and the arboretum. His idea was to create a living museum of tree and shrub species, both native and exotic, and group them according to plant family. Between 1934 and 1941 immense plantings were installed at the arboretum surrounding the formal gardens.

During the war years, collection plantings came to a standstill while the Victory Garden program took center stage and families in the Milwaukee area competed for prizes in growing the biggest and best vegetables in the Root River Parkway public gardens. Plantings resumed in the formal garden area during the 1950s and early '60s with the establishment of the Herb Garden, the Test Gardens, and the Hedge Garden.

In 1974 much of the nature education was taken over by the Wehr Nature Center, and a prairie restoration project, begun in 1965, became a part of this center.

TOP. *In the late 1930s Alfred L. Boerner, landscape architect for the Milwaukee County Park system, believed that Whitnall Park should offer not only natural areas but formal gardens as well.*

ABOVE. *Taking advantage of the sweeping vistas of the surrounding landscape, Boerner designed the Botanical Gardens to resemble a garden on a European estate.*

A quiet pool reflecting the surrounding plants is found next to the small stone house used as a visitors' center and gift shop.

Statues in the Gardens are 1930s products of the WPA (Works Projects Administration). Many of the artists who participated in this program later went on to gain national recognition for their work. Jeff Greer designed the boy and girl statues in the Annual Garden; George Adams Dietrich designed the statue of a mother and two sons in the Perennial Garden; and the two small animal sculptures at the entrance to the Garden House were done by James Gehr.

The formal gardens at Boerner Botanical Gardens are laid out in an L shape, with the Walled Garden serving as the pivotal point. To the west lie the Perennial Garden and the Rose Garden, and to the south are found the Shrub Mall and the Rock Garden.

The Trial Garden serves as part of the All-America Selections testing program and is educational as well as beautiful. Here new cultivars grow side by side with old favorites, showing the brightest colors of the season. On the average, 26,000 annuals are planted in this area each year.

West of the Walled Garden, the long borders of the Perennial Garden are planted with over 9,900 perennial plants. Both professionals and home gardeners come away from this area with new ideas of species and cultivars that do well in this region. Benches along the walks make this a good place to sit and soak up the sun after a long Wisconsin winter.

At the end of the Perennial Garden is the Rose Garden, where America's favorite flower is displayed. All kinds of roses are on show here, from tree roses to miniatures, old-fashioned favorites to the most unusual and newest cultivars developed by rosarians—over 350 different kinds of roses, including a wonderful collection of climbing roses that grow on a series of arbors. In the center of this garden is a large pool that holds Boerner's collection of water lilies. Each June, the Friends of Boerner Botanical Garden host a rose festival. The nine-day event, free to the public, features entertainment, educational lectures, and exhibits.

TOP. *Boerner Botanical Gardens display roses of every shape and form, in all imaginable colors.*

ABOVE. *The intricate and delicate beauty of these flowers never fails to delight the rose lover.*

OPPOSITE. *America's favorite flower is displayed in the Rose Garden, site of the annual Friends of Boerner Botanical Gardens Rose Festival.*

Vegetables and herbs are grown in a formal area, demonstrating that plants can be both beautiful and useful.

At the edge of the Rose Garden, sweeping vistas of the surrounding Whitnall Park provide a feeling of being at an immense country estate. Huge lawns are dotted with trees that make up the Arboretum's collection.

The Herb Garden, first planted in 1952, displays herbaceous plants suitable for use in cooking, crafts, and medicine. Interpretive labels in this area of the garden tell the common and scientific names of the various plants and explain how the plants are used.

East of the Herb Garden is Boerner's daylily collection, making this area a colorful sight during summer months. Parallel to the daylily collection is the Shrub Mall, composed of many different kinds, both deciduous, evergreen, and flowering shrubs. Chief among these are yews, tree peonies, and junipers. At the end of the Shrub Mall is the Rock Garden, originally planted in 1941. Today it is composed of a limestone grotto planted with native Wisconsin wildflowers.

The Peony Garden, close to the Garden House, puts on a beautiful show in late spring as these sweet-smelling plants color the landscape with their pink, red, and white petals. Over 350 different varieties fill the beds, lining closely clipped grass lawns.

The Arboretum of the Boerner Botanical Gardens encompasses about 1,000 acres. Native trees and

OPPOSITE. *The combination of formal flower beds, extensive plantings of trees, and sweeping vistas delight thousands of visitors each year at Boerner Botanical Gardens.*

shrubs as well as species from other countries, and old specimens as well as young seedlings, grow here. Several oaks and maples date from the 1750s. Perhaps the best known of all the collections is the planting of crabapples, begun in 1933. Today it includes about 250 species and varieties and is considered the largest such collection in this country.

The tree and shrub collections found closest to the Botanical Gardens include magnolia, viburnum, ornamental cherry and plum, hydrangea, and dogwood. Interspersed among these collections are tulips which carpet the area with 21,000 blossoms in spring.

Today Boerner Botanical Gardens is a spectacularly beautiful park. The combination of formal gardens with large expanses of natural areas provides vistas that delight thousands of visitors annually.

The personalities, dreams, and visions of these two men, Alfred Boerner and Charles Whitnall, have resulted in a unique and beautiful park that offers opportunities for education and inspiration to all visitors. As Alfred Boerner said, "It is not only for us, but for our children and grandchildren who will reap the full benefit."

Arthur Ode, noted horticulturist who served as first assistant director of the Botanical Gardens, once said, "We must first learn to take care of our own backyards if we are to learn to take care of the world." If this is true, Milwaukee County is well on its way to doing its share of taking care of the world.

Cleveland Botanical Garden

Cleveland, Ohio

THE CLEVELAND BOTANICAL GARDEN is a small, green jewel in the heart of downtown Cleveland. Neighboring buildings house the Cleveland Art Museum, the Natural History Museum, and Severance Hall. This small garden covers only seven acres, but the displays are wonderful, and the garden strives to maintain the original purpose of the founders, of educating the people of Cleveland in the art of horticulture.

What's in a name? Is a rose sweeter by any other name? No, and neither is a botanical garden, but the correct name tells much about what a garden is all about. In 1933 when the garden was first founded, it was called the Garden Center of Greater Cleveland. In the years since then, the term "garden center" more often referred to a shop where flowers and shrubs are sold rather than a place to delight and educate gardeners about plants.

In the words of Donald W. Morrison, president of the board of trustees, "I believe we will better reach the public and better serve them, bearing a corporate name that clearly suggests the kind of programs we embrace and the objectives of education and service we pursue." In 1994 the name was officially changed to the Cleveland Botanical Garden.

Brian E. Holley, executive director of the Garden, identifies four main goals for the future: to continue developing programs and activities in urban horticulture to further the "greening" of the city; to provide heightened information services (such as the library and the horticulture phone

The Western Reserve Herb Garden at Cleveland Botanical Garden is world-renowned for its design and collection of plants.

This 1923 photograph shows the first building for the Cleveland Botanical Garden, a boathouse at the edge of a lagoon near the Cleveland Museum of Art.

line); to emphasize public programs; and to develop and document the horticultural collections.

The idea of a botanical garden for the city of Cleveland came to life in January 1930 at the home of Mrs. William G. Mather, president of the Garden Club of Cleveland. The club was meeting once again to discuss something that was becoming an increasingly difficult problem—what to do with the extensive horticultural library donated to them by one of their members, Mrs. Andrew Squire. The books had been housed at the Cleveland Museum of Art for years, but crowded conditions there made it clear that this valuable collection needed a permanent home.

Surrounding the art museum was a public park that included a pond where citizens skated during winter months and boated during the summer. An old abandoned boathouse at the edge of the lagoon had formerly served as shelter for boaters.

Mrs. Walter White, head of the library commit-tee, suggested that they place the books in the boat-house, and it was decided that the horticultural library would be housed there and that it would be called a garden center. In the words of Mrs. White, "From that time, developments have proceeded with breathtaking rapidity."

The Garden Club of Cleveland launched into their Garden Center project with unabashed enthusi-asm. In June 1930 the group hosted a "French Street Fair" and raised $17,000 to refurbish the boathouse and make it into a garden center.

The Garden Center opened to the public on December 4, 1930, and during the first month hosted one thousand visitors. The boathouse was trans-formed to a place of beauty complete with exhibition room, office, library, and dressing rooms.

In her report on the first year, Mrs. William Mather wrote, "On the second floor is a quiet little library containing over 500 volumes and ever-growing files pertaining to flowers, gardens and various phases

The Garden Club of Cleveland
held its first fund-raising
White Elephant Sale in 1933,
with proceeds then, as now,
going toward the support of the
Botanical Garden.

of horticulture and nature . . . this [is] a delightful spot where garden lovers may browse or search undisturbed for garden information."

Volunteers at the Garden Center were quick to share their knowledge and information. In 1933, to help pay for the many programs sponsored by the Center, the Garden Club of Cleveland held its first White Elephant Sale, an event that has been held every year since then. In 1936 the Center turned its attention toward children and began its long association with the Cleveland Public Schools. Through the years thousands of children have greatly benefited from the association with the Garden.

The grounds at the Center were also developed. In the mid-1940s a rooftop garden was created; it included a formal deck garden, Italian loggia garden, well garden, yellow garden, blue garden, and a white garden.

The Garden Center of Greater Cleveland, as it was renamed in 1933, has the distinction of being one of the first such centers in the United States. It is predated only by the garden center begun a year earlier in Hackensack, New Jersey. By 1939 the *Cleveland Plain Dealer* was to report that "in the last decade 140 similar garden centers have been established by different communities in the U.S. Most of them are patterned after and inspired by the Cleveland institute."

Nineteen fifty-nine brought a flood with a silver lining to the Garden Center. On June 1, water from a flash flood entered the Garden Center building at street level and spilled down the stairs to the first floor. As torrents of water washed out the staircase, volunteers rescued the valuable horticultural books, stacking them on top of chairs and tables and high shelves.

Damage to the reconstructed boathouse was severe and the decision was made to move the Garden Center rather than repair the building. The site chosen for the new building was just up the hill and not far away on a site formerly occupied by the

Cleveland Zoo. A small wooden building that had served as the monkey house still remained on the property; the lovely ravine had, at one time, been home to the bears.

The old boathouse building was once again abandoned, but not forgotten. Many mementoes from the boathouse were incorporated into the new building, including the chandeliers from the entrance lobby. The statue of St. Fiacre, patron saint of gardeners, which was originally in the roof garden, now resides in the Garden Room.

The grounds surrounding the new building were planted with a "garland of gardens," the first of which was the Herb Garden. Dedicated in September 1969, the Herb Garden was the special project of the Western Reserve Herb Society, a unit of the Herb Society of America. They presented it to "the people of Cleveland and to all people for Health, for Goodness, and for Beauty."

The Herb Garden was quickly followed by the Rose Garden, dedicated in November 1971. In 1973 the Reading Garden was completed, and in 1975 the Japanese Garden was added.

The most recent addition is the Wildflower Garden, which provides a uniquely secluded woodland trail in this urban area.

Outside the long Garden Center building, anchored on one end by Clark Hall and on the other by the library, two lily pools and a landscaped terrace provide a beautiful entrance to both the building and the gardens.

The largest and most dramatic of all the garden areas is the Western Reserve Herb Garden, world-renowned for its design and its collection of plants. An earlier herb garden was established on this site in the mid-1940s and was maintained by members of the Western Reserve Herb Society. In 1969 a new garden was planned based on an agreement between the Herb Society and the Garden Center. The garden was designed by Elsetta Gilchrist Barnes, who was influenced both by the original herb garden and by the new Garden Center building. The new herb garden, encompassing an area 160 feet by ninety feet, is a formal design made up of geometric beds. In the center is a stunning knot garden that has come to represent not only the Herb Garden but the Botanical Garden itself. Ribbons of small gray and green hedges are intertwined to create a "knot" effect, a design popular in England during the sixteenth century. In Cleveland, this design is accomplished with shrubs such as dwarf boxwood, lavender, gray and green santolina, germander, and crimson thyme. These plants wind in and around five millstones, each of which measures six feet across.

South of the knot garden are the trial and cutting gardens, providing the Herb Society with the fresh and dried materials that they need for making crafts and gifts for an annual fund-raising sale. One of the two beds found here is devoted to trying new cultivars, or in experimenting with growing herbs not usually cultivated in this region. This experimental bed is one of the favorites in the garden, for it provides a living education for both visitors and scholars. Plants in the trial and cutting gardens change from one year to the next, though old stand-bys are always found here. Plants such as onion, yarrow, thyme, basil, lavender, sage, and germander can be counted on to provide a beautiful display year after year.

The Dye Garden, found at the southwestern corner of the Herb Garden, is full of plants that historically have been used to color cloth or yarn. Nearly every color of the rainbow can be created from natural dyes found in these plants. These include many herbs one would expect, such as onion, dyers woad, and madder, but also include some surprising species such as lily-of-the-valley and Queen Anne's lace. Annuals, perennials, trees, and shrubs provide pigments used for dyeing.

A long allee of historical and species roses pays homage to this queen of all plants, which has been

The Herb Garden encompasses an area 160 feet by 90 feet and is a formal design with geometric beds filled with flowers and herbs used for flavoring, dyeing, and medicine.

used for centuries for flavoring and fragrance. The Culinary Garden holds the usual parsley, sage, rosemary, and thyme, but also some showy ornamentals whose presence proves that utility and beauty are not mutually exclusive. Two central beds are filled with salad herbs and it is a place where touching, rubbing, and sniffing leaves is certainly encouraged.

Medicinal plants have been essential to every civilization, our own included. The Medicinal Garden is a tribute to plants that stifle sniffles, quiet coughs, and relieve headaches. Both the common medicinal plants, such as chamomile, used to soothe a baby's upset stomach, and scientifically critical ones such as tropical periwinkle, crucial to the treatment of leukemia, are found growing here, making this

garden a popular one with students and faculty from nearby hospitals.

North of the Herb Garden is the Rose Garden, designed by Charles L. Knight. Both old-fashioned roses and the newest cultivars are grown here. During early summer, thousands of blossoms turn this corner of the garden into a maze of color and fragrance.

The Reading Garden was built outside the library. A gazebo, pergola, and wooden benches create comfortable places to sit and read or study. In this area, annuals, perennials, bulbs, trees, and shrubs make for year-round beauty.

Stone steps leading from the Reading Garden bring the visitor down to the Japanese Garden, a gift to Cleveland Botanical Garden from members of

The Rose Garden displays both old-fashioned and new varieties of these enchanting flowers.

Ikebana International Cleveland Chapter Twenty. The garden combines two distinct styles of Japanese landscape design, the dry landscape and the tea garden. Built into a hillside, the garden is best viewed from under the trellis at the entrance.

A stone lantern surrounded by hostas and rhododendrons sets the stage. Originally used as temple lights, stone lanterns were only later employed as garden ornaments. Conifers, such as umbrella pine, Carolina hemlock, false cypress, and dawn redwood, form the background for azaleas, rhododendrons, and other smaller plants.

The focal point of the garden, called *Gan Ryuu Tei,* "rock stream garden," is a collection of shrubs, boulders, and weathered beach stones arranged to give the illusion of a mountain stream. A dry pool was installed at the base of the cascade in 1992. Like many other Japanese gardens, this is to be viewed from a distance.

From the entrance to the Japanese Garden the visitor can also enter the Wildflower Garden, a woodland trail planted with wildflowers native to the midwestern United States. This garden reaches its height of beauty in spring.

Even though the Cleveland Botanical Garden, originally known as the Garden Center of Greater Cleveland, is located in the heart of the city, it offers a place of peace and solitude.

ABOVE. *Cleveland Botanical Garden remains dedicated to the concepts of learning about plants and nurturing them.*

OPPOSITE. *In the Japanese Garden the* Gan Ryuu Tei *("rock stream garden") is arranged to give the illusion of a mountain stream.*

Throughout its long history, the Cleveland Botanical Garden, described as a place for learning and growing, has remained true to the principles of its founders. In its outreach programs to the school system and a new dedication to the art and science of horticulture therapy, the Cleveland Botanical Garden is changing people's lives.

A brochure on therapeutic gardening published by the Garden is dedicated to "discovering that the love and care of plants nurtures the gardener as well," a sentiment that may well explain why the Garden Center, established in Cleveland, Ohio, in 1930, was the precursor for hundreds of such centers established in the United States. The union of plants and people will forever result in that magic called a garden, where the care of plants nurtures the soul.

Michigan State University Horticultural Demonstration Gardens*

East Lansing, Michigan

THERE ARE UNDOUBTEDLY many beautiful college campuses in the United States. Few can compare, however, to the acres of gardens found on the campus of Michigan State University (MSU).

The horticultural tradition at Michigan State is rich. Graduates from the school include famous plantsmen such as Liberty Hyde Bailey and William James Beal. These men set early standards of excellence that are still effective today.

Since its beginning as the Michigan State College of Agriculture, the institution has placed strong emphasis on the beautification of the grounds. In 1946 President John Hannah created the Division of Campus Park and Planning, now composed of professional landscape architects, horticulturists, and botanists. The entire 5,500 acres of the campus were considered a park, which now has 1,500 different species and 260 cultivars of flowering crabapples, making it one of the largest collections in North America.

The newest gardens, developed at the south end of campus, are colorful jewels in the rich grandeur of a campus already renowned for its beauty.

In 1986 the Department of Horticulture moved to a new building on the south campus. The Plant and Soil Sciences Building provided more space and much-needed updated teaching and research facilities. At this time it was decided that the gardens surrounding the old horticulture buildings would be maintained as a park, and that new display gardens would be created next to the new building. This decision initially made a lot of people unhappy. Tom Kehler, director of MSU's Campus Park and Planning, recalls that people kept asking who was going to visit a garden all the way over on the south campus.

It's a question no one asks anymore. Since construction first began on this garden in 1989, hundreds of thousands of visitors from all over the world have found their way to the display gardens on the south campus.

Many people doubted that the gardens would ever amount to much because the site was so poor. Heavy bulldozers used during the construction of the buildings and a severe drought during the summer of 1988 resulted in hard, compacted soils. But the dreamers and planners were undaunted, and by the spring of 1989 small wooden stakes were "planted" on the garden site, marking the placement of walks, beds, and landscaping features.

Money for the garden was raised by pledges from a cross-section of people, including alumni, garden lovers, and professionals from the horticultural industry. Over two million dollars was raised, most of which was pledged over a five-year period, meaning that the garden could not be built all at once. Construction, begun in 1989, was not finished until 1993.

Dr. William Carlton, a professor of horticulture, was faculty coordinator of the gardens. "I like to define the gardens as a laboratory where plants and people grow together. This garden fulfills its mission, as it informs people that plants not only contain an element of beauty, but of necessity."

The plants on display at the Horticultural Demonstration Gardens most certainly contain an element of necessity, but thousands upon thousands of colorful blossoms make the element of beauty almost overwhelming. All this beauty provides a stunning outdoor classroom in which students obtain hands-on experience in the art and science of horticulture.

The campus of Michigan State University is blessed with a multitude of gardens, offering students the opportunity to learn both the science of horticulture and the magic of gardening.

All-America Selection test beds for perennials, roses, and such annuals as these petunias are located at the south end of the campus.

Students are responsible for planting and maintaining the gardens and the greenhouses, acquiring both practical and academic knowledge.

The seven and a half acres that make up the gardens are divided into five distinct gardens: Perennial Garden, Annual Trial Garden, Foyer Garden, Rose Garden, and the Idea Garden. The entrance to the gardens is tended by Wilbir, a fourteen-foot floral peacock.

The Entrance Pavilion is shaded by vine-covered wooden trellises. The vine of choice for this area is hyacinth bean, *Dolichos lablab,* an annual vine that produces pinkish-lavender blossoms and reddish-violet seedpods and always draws rave reviews from visitors. A trailing begonia, "Spartan Beauty," was developed at MSU by Dr. Lowell Euart. It was introduced to the general nursery trade at the time of the grand opening of the Horticultural Demonstration Gardens, and is now grown in hanging baskets taking center stage at the Pavilion.

From the Entrance Pavilion, visitors can look out over the Perennial Garden, made up of ten island planting beds filled with colorful perennials. In all, nearly 6,000 square feet of bed space are planted with these flowers, bulbs, and ornamental grasses that bloom year after year. Laura Coit, horticulturist at MSU, designed the perennial plantings and chose plant material carefully. Her goal was to inspire interest in perennials by choosing a wide range of plants that not only look beautiful when in bloom, but also provide color, texture, or interesting foliage from April to December. For the most part, these plants were chosen with the home gardener in mind and display the wonderful variety available in these plants. Although most of the perennials grown in this garden today require full sun for optimum growth, by the late 1990s it is hoped that strategically planted trees will provide enough shade to allow for display of shade-loving perennials as well.

Many perennials found in this garden were moved here from the old horticultural garden next to the original horticulture hall. Old-fashioned favorites such as daylilies, iris, chrysanthemums, and phlox are grown beside lesser-known perennials, offering the visitor a chance to experience a bit of the familiar along with the new. Even well-known flowers take on a new twist as different cultivars and hybrids are developed. Gardeners can see which plants, both old and new, perform well in this region. The perennial pond, a focal point in the garden, shows water lilies and other aquatic plants which can be grown in a home water garden.

Next to the Perennial Garden, the Rose Garden is composed of three circular beds connected with walks and white arbors. This garden is an All-America Selections Rose Trial Garden. Many plants grown here are "on trial" for two years to determine qualities such as foliage, color, and plant habit as well as their resistance to disease and pests. Each year, trial roses are planted and are evaluated twice, once during the summer and again in fall. They are then left to overwinter in the garden and are evaluated twice

Hyacinth bean (Dolichos lablab) *is an annual vine that covers the wooden trellises at the Entrance Pavilion leading to the Horticultural Demonstration Gardens.*

more the second year. Results are sent to the All-America Rose Selections committee; generally, the winners are introduced to the market two to three years later.

Along with the test plants, 700 display roses delight and educate visitors.

The Annual Trial Garden is designed in a formal neoclassic style, complete with sunken garden, fountain, and gazebo. The intensity of colors in this garden is memorable. Each year over 1,000 new and recently introduced annual cultivars are tested in this garden. The All-America Selections entries grown in the test gardens are not yet available to the general public, but are sent to thirty-three different official test gardens throughout the United States and Canada to be evaluated for beauty and ease of growing. The MSU Horticultural Demonstration Gardens are proud to be part of this program.

New cultivars are planted next to familiar favorites, resulting in over 35,000 annuals in this garden every year, grown from seeds sent from all over the world. The cultivars grown include from fifty to one hundred and fifty samples each of petunias, pansies, impatiens, fibrous-rooted begonias, marigolds, and seed-geraniums. The annuals are evaluated on qualities such as height, color, uniformity of growth, disease resistance, and vigor. In August a Seedman's Field Day is hosted when seed growers come to see their seeds "all grown up," and to evaluate for themselves which new creations will be worth introducing to the public.

Although it is interesting to see new cultivars growing even before they are available to the general public, the amazing sight of 35,000 annuals all growing together in one garden is reason enough to visit this garden in late summer.

The Annual Trial Garden is home to two pieces of statuary. A life-sized sculpture of Liberty Hyde Bailey—a graduate of Michigan State College of Agriculture and the father of American horticulture—is found at the eastern end of the annual garden under the arch. The other statue, called *Sunseed,* is a stainless-steel piece sculpted by another graduate of MSU, Owen Vernon Shaffer.

The Foyer Garden is a "teaser"; clearly visible from outside the gardens, it gives passersby a small glimpse of what is in store for them through the garden gate.

The last garden in the complex is the Idea Garden, where twelve ten-by-thirty-five-foot plots are filled to bursting with creative and innovative ideas about home gardening. Each year a different theme is adopted, often including ideas on heritage vegetables, composting, and dried flowers.

Used for the All-America Selections vegetable trials, this garden is maintained in part by volunteers from the Michigan Master Gardening program. Individuals spearhead different projects, such as growing heirloom (nonhybrid) tomatoes, or unusual fruits and flowers.

Next to the Horticultural Demonstration Gardens are teaching greenhouses, used for both student projects and for growing bedding plants. The botany greenhouses, at the north end of Farm Lane near the old horticultural gardens, offer various tours on subjects such as pollination, plant survival, plants from around the world, and butterflies.

The Horticultural Demonstration Gardens at Michigan State University were created to teach and to inspire visitors and students. They accomplish these goals admirably; in fact, the casual visitor is often so inspired he or she soon displays the classic behavior of a student—closely inspecting the plants, reading labels, and taking notes. Likewise, the university student, unable to contain his or her amazement at the breathtaking beauty of this living laboratory, stands like a tourist and stares in wonder at this fairyland of flowers.

W. J. Beal Botanical Garden

Michigan State University Campus, East Lansing, Michigan

MANY GREAT BOTANICAL gardens have had humble beginnings, but perhaps none more so than the now esteemed W. J. Beal Botanical Garden on the campus of Michigan State University.

In 1873 Professor William J. Beal decided he wanted a place where his students could study nature firsthand. To accomplish this end, he planted some 140 species of native or naturalized grasses and clovers in a ravine near the Red Cedar River on campus. His "weed patches" were so useful for teaching purposes and drew so much attention from campus visitors that Beal decided to expand his little garden, and in 1877 he installed many other kinds of plants,

including wildflowers, shrubs, annuals, and perennials. Beal's outdoor laboratory has continued to grow both in size and stature over the last century. Today it encompasses over five acres and includes more than 5,000 different kinds of plants.

Even though Beal's garden has gained an international reputation for excellence, it is still basically a teaching garden, a fact that would please its founder. William J. Beal was an outstanding botanist, horticulturist, and research scientist, but more than anything else he was a wonderful teacher.

Beal was born in Lenawee County, Michigan, in 1833. Always interested in the sciences, he graduated from the University of Michigan in 1859 and entered Harvard in 1861. He spent his first ten weeks there studying chemistry, but he soon realized that it was not to his liking, since he considered "book lessons" boring. He switched to the study of botany and zoology and studied under two outstanding professors, Asa Gray and Louis Agassiz. These two men had completely different methods of teaching. Agassiz was a "hands-on" man, and required his students to spend months observing and sketching before he gave them any formal instruction or allowed them to use textbooks. Asa Gray, on the other hand, depended almost entirely on textbook lessons and formal lectures. Years later Beal was to say that both men influenced his own teaching methods. "I think the true course lies between the two."

Upon receiving a bachelor of science degree from Harvard, Beal taught for several years before being hired as professor of botany and horticultural at Michigan State College of Agriculture in 1870.

He was quick to make a lasting impression on his students. Remembering his experiences at Harvard, Beal combined the hands-on approach of Agassiz with the traditional teaching methods of Gray. He required his students to collect and study plants carefully, and to describe in their own words the characteristics of each specimen. He was there to help and give advice in class, though, and even allowed the students to use textbooks after a few weeks.

One student told him later, "I remember well that you gave me a pea vine and kept me studying it for three days before telling me anything. I now consider it the most valuable lesson I ever learned from anyone."

Beal considered it crucial to the learning process for his students to observe for themselves. When a student voiced his frustration that he didn't see anything, Beal would utter a phrase for which he soon became famous: "Keep on squinting." He was adamant that his students depend on their own powers of observation and said, "To be constantly

Professor William J. Beal started a botanical garden in 1873 to give his students a place to observe nature. His first "weed patch" has grown into an outdoor laboratory that now displays over 5,000 kinds of plants.

giving information in science makes intellectual tramps, and not trained investigators." The students fortunate enough to study with Beal became trained investigators.

Beal's son-in-law once said of him, "I learned from him the one thing I needed most of all to know. This was to look at life before I talked about it; not to look at it second-hand, by the way of books, but so far as possible to examine the thing itself, and form my own conclusions about it."

Beal wanted his students to be able to observe plants quickly and easily, and thus he decided to create a botanical garden. Instead of waiting for funds that would allow him to create a grand garden, Beal simply found a spot of land on campus and began planting grasses and clovers. He wrote, "I thought a very small garden would do just as well to experiment with till experience had enabled me to make a few mistakes."

Beal depended on his students to supply much of the labor necessary for the garden, including help from his student, Liberty Hyde Bailey, now considered the father of American horticulture. In 1928 Bailey said of the botanical garden, "The site chosen—along the banks of a little stream flowing into the Red Cedar River—was fortunate. Probably no better place on the campus could have been chosen to furnish the various conditions of growth required by such an assemblage of plants."

The original idea of the garden was to grow the common plants and weeds together for easy observation. Later developments resulted in plant families being grouped together, a was common in many European botanical gardens. Aesthetic groupings were at this time not considered, so for many years the garden was called the "wild garden."

Although Beal was deeply interested in the botanical garden which he had started, his contributions did not stop there. Having read Charles Darwin's scientific paper on cross-breeding in the vegetable kingdom, Beal began his breeding experiments on corn. In 1877 he became the first to cross-fertilize corn, resulting in increased yields through hybrid vigor, helping to make corn one of the most important crops grown in the United States.

Beal's scientific curiosity outlived him. In 1879 he declared that he wished to learn more about how long seeds would remain viable. To satisfy his curiosity, Beal selected fifty seeds of twenty different common weeds and mixed them with sandy soil placed in twenty small glass bottles. The bottles were buried at a depth of eighteen inches, their mouths tilted at an angle to prevent water from entering them.

The plan was to dig up a bottle every five years and test the germination of the seeds. In 1920 the time period was changed to ten years, and later to even longer time periods to prolong the experiment. In 1980—a century after the experiment was begun— seeds from the common moth mullein, *Verbascum blattaria,* still germinated.

The garden grew year by year until, at Beal's retirement in 1910, it contained over 2,100 species of plants. Soon after his retirement, great changes were made in the garden. Water features found on the grounds of the garden— the small brook, bogs, and pond—became so polluted that they were drained or channeled underground.

The garden continued to grow. By 1928 it was a part of a network of gardens participating in an international seed exchange, and no fewer than 800 plants were grown from seeds sent from around the world. Not surprisingly, many of these plants were being grown in central Michigan for the first time.

In 1950 the garden was redefined and expanded by Professor Milton Baron, campus landscape architect. In spite of changes, great effort was made to retain Beal's original concept of the garden. Dr. George Parmalee, long-time curator of the garden, said that "Hannah [then president of the University] was concerned that the garden was leaning toward a horticultural perspective rather than botanical, and he felt that was not what Professor Beal had intended. A horticultural garden tends to emphasize plants with distinctive color. While we don't reject plants because of their color, neither do we emphasize it."

Walking into the garden today is like walking into a living botany textbook. The first thing the visitor notices is a sea of signs, each neatly labeling

RIGHT. *A wood anemone* (Anemone quinquefolia) *at right and a spring beauty* (Claytonia virginica).

OPPOSITE. *Walking into the garden today is like walking into a living botany textbook. An extensive labeling system identifies plants by common and botanical names.*

the plants and giving both botanical and common names. The labeling system was introduced by Beal in the very beginning. He wrote in his 1910 report to the university, "From observation I learn that very few visitors even stop to read a label; yet if some plants are not labeled for a few weeks, some complaints are heard."

The garden is divided into different "chapters" so that both academic and casual students can learn quickly and easily. There are four main groups: Plant Families, Useful Plants, Forest Communities, and Landscape Plants.

The Plant Families collection is grouped according to botanical family and plants are displayed by evolutionary development. The Useful Plant collection is made up of species that have had an economic impact, either beneficial or detrimental. Beneficial plants are grouped according to purpose and include plants used for dyes, fiber, flavoring, medicine, perfume, and food—vegetables and their wild relatives. Also included in this section are special groups including oil plants, honey plants, and North American Indian food plants.

Plants with a negative economic influence include those poisonous to livestock, and weeds. Beal loved almost all plants but he had a particular aversion to weeds such as quack grass. Raised a Quaker, Beal was said to have had three enemies in life—"alcohol, tobacco, and quack grass."

The Forest Communities collection includes trees, shrubs, and wildflowers that occur naturally in Michigan and the eastern United States. One of the most important exhibits in this area displays species that are endangered or threatened in Michigan. Established in 1988 by the curator, Dr. Gerard Donnelly, plants in the collection are marked according to their endangerment status: Extirpated (plants known to have been native to the state but which are now believed to be extinct there); Endangered (plants in danger of becoming extinct in Michigan); Threatened (plants likely to become endangered if

In the garden, plants are divided into four main groups: Plant Families, Useful Plants, Forest Communities, and Landscape Plants.

protective measures are not taken); and Special Concern (plants identified by the Department of Natural Resources as needing special attention).

Plants such as Jacob's ladder, *Polemonium reptans,* and Houghton's goldenrod, *Solidago houghtonii,* are exhibited here.

The Landscape Collection includes plants of ornamental value planted together for aesthetic appeal. Of particular beauty is the collection of rhododendrons and azaleas that make Beal Botanical Garden an exciting place to see in spring and early summer.

Beal Botanical Garden is ever-changing, moving naturally in directions that make it even more valuable to those students who read in the leaves and flowers the story of plants, how they arrived and evolved, how human destiny is inextricably dependent on their destiny. The lessons to be learned from the plants are diverse and far-reaching, for the future of plants, both common and rare, abundant and endangered, is forever tied to our own.

4-H Children's Garden
Michigan State University, East Lansing, Michigan

IF YOU'VE EVER wondered what it would be to walk through the Hundred Acre Woods like Winnie-the-Pooh, or wander through a maze like Alice in Wonderland, come to the 4-H Children's Garden on the campus of Michigan State University and let your imagination run wild. This half-acre plot of magic was created just for children, but luckily adults are allowed to tag along. The brainchild of an energetic and enthusiastic 4-H Children's Garden curator, Jane Taylor, this garden is not only educational but fun.

The Garden was designed by landscape architects, Jeffrey Kacos and Deborah Kinney, in Michigan State University's Division of Campus Park and Planning. The design was brought to life by Jane

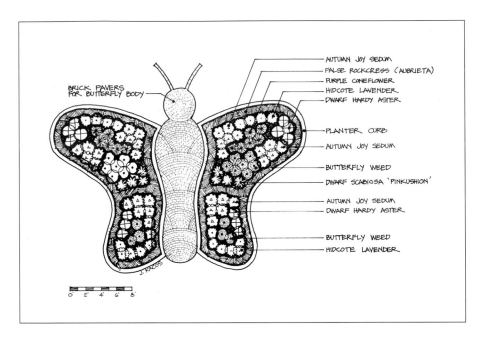

AUTUMN JOY SEDUM
FALSE ROCKCRESS (AUBRIETA)
PURPLE CONEFLOWER
HIDCOTE LAVENDER
DWARF HARDY ASTER

BRICK PAVERS
FOR BUTTERFLY BODY

PLANTER CURB
AUTUMN JOY SEDUM

BUTTERFLY WEED

DWARF SCABIOSA 'PINKUSHION'

AUTUMN JOY SEDUM
DWARF HARDY ASTER

BUTTERFLY WEED
HIDCOTE LAVENDER

0 2' 4' 6' 8'

The Butterfly Garden, with a brick paver body and flower wings, includes plants which serve to feed both caterpillars and butterflies.

Taylor and her colleagues, who filled this small garden with the most creative ideas imaginable—and all with the young, and the young at heart, in mind.

Many of the ideas came from children themselves. When youngsters enrolled in the MSU Laboratory School were asked if they liked to visit gardens, they turned up their noses and grumbled that gardens were boring and were only for grown-ups. Okay, then, what would you like to see in a garden? they were asked.

The kids couldn't talk fast enough and the first (and most repeated) request—no "NO!" signs, no "Do Not Touch!" signs. Jane and the staff began taking notes.

"We want a tree house, Peter Rabbit's garden, a crayon garden, dinosaurs, butterflies and a beanstalk for Jack to climb." Their excitement was contagious, and the Michigan 4-H Foundation began raising money. This was going to be good.

And it is good. The 4-H Children's Garden at MSU may be the most creative half-acre in America. Visitors are greeted at the entrance by huge mother and baby teddy-bear topiaries, with arms outstretched. Kids walk up to these five-foot-tall bears made of English ivy, creeping fig, and babies' tears, and grandparents instantly realize that this is a great photo opportunity. The cameras generally keep clicking for the remainder of the visit.

Once the kids finally leave the teddy bears, they travel under "Imagination Arbor" and into the Garden. Because the entire garden is enclosed with a fence and created with children in mind, it is a safe and happy place for children to visit. As adults stand at the ABC Garden—which begins with aster and ends with zinnia—and identify the plants whose names begin with every letter in between, the children are off to explore, pausing only long enough to watch the miniature train that travels through the area.

The tree house draws kids like a magnet. The main structure is made from peeled limbs of white cedar and the "walls" are made of rope woven into spiderweb designs. From this lofty perch it is possible to view the entire garden.

The Dinosaur Garden is complete with plants that grew in the time of the dinosaurs and includes a ginkgo tree, ferns, and scouring rushes; it features a huge topiary Stegosaurus. Kids are encouraged to crawl through a metal dinosaur rib cage covered with the vines from "Dinosaur" gourd. A sand pit contains plant fossils that the kids dig up over and over again.

A figure-eight pond is spanned by a replica of the green bridge found in Claude Monet's Garden. The ponds are complete with fountains that spray giant spurts of water and bubble fountains low enough for young children to touch.

A swinging gate proves to be irresistible to kids who like to hang on things, and they are welcome to do so. Much to their delight, an extra surprise is in store for all those who pull on the gate. Every time the gate swings open, two bronze frogs in the center of the pond squirt a long spray of water in their direction.

Alice in Wonderland's maze is made from a cedar hedge. For those who find the center (and of course nearly everyone does), a special treat is in store. What else but a Secret Garden complete

with a statue of Mary Lennox, a character from the popular children's novel *The Secret Garden*.

The Scarecrow Garden contains a wonderful metal scarecrow sculpture at the end of a golden brick road, around which are planted poppies and three different kinds of pumpkins named 'Munchkin', 'Oz', and 'Wizard'.

The Enchanted Garden includes plants such as Peter Pan squash and Thumbelina zinnia, while the zoological garden displays spiderplant, lamb's ears, and other "animal plants."

The Pizza Garden is round, and divided into "slices," in which grows everything needed for a pizza—including tomatoes, peppers, basil, and even yellow marigolds for "cheese."

Consistent with the children's request for no "No" signs, markers in several parts of the garden ask children to "Please gently touch." Many of these signs are found in the "Sense-Ational" Herb Garden,

Two giant topiaries of bears give an open-armed welcome to visitors at Michigan State's 4-H Children's Garden. Surely one of the most creatively planted places on earth, this garden is both fun and educational.

4 - H C h i l d r e n ' s G a r d e n

A walk-in sundial, Pizza Garden, swinging gate, and Peter Rabbit's Garden make the Children's Garden a delightful experience for all ages.

the Perfume Garden, Peter Rabbit's Garden, and the Performing Plants Garden—where kids learn that plants such as impatiens and mimosa really *do* things.

The Scientific Discovery Garden shows many new plant cultivars developed by scientists at MSU. Turf from the field in the Pontiac Silver Dome where the 1994 World Cup Soccer tournament was played also grows here, along with a moth mullein plant grown from a seed buried over a hundred years ago by William J. Beal. Not to be outdone by a mere adult, children perform their own "Seeds for the Future" time capsule seed experiment and bury seeds from tomatoes, cabbage, and mullein in a stainless-steel capsule. One capsule will be opened every ten years until 2093 to determine which seeds will still germinate.

The Garden is a hands-on, feet-on, arms-on environment. One of the most popular spots is the Dance Chime, where a series of three rows of brass plates make musical tones when the children step on them. The area surrounding the chimes are naturally planted with varieties such as Trumpet vine, 'Piccolo' cosmos, and 'Melody' spinach.

In a different area a walk-in sundial allows children to tell what time it is by raising their arms and observing the shadow cast on the hour block. Plantings include four o'clocks and thyme.

The bowl-shaped Cereal Garden grows plants found in a morning cereal bowl: corn, oats, wheat, and rice. A 900-pound bronze-and-epoxy sheep looks over a tiny pasture featuring plants which provide us with milk, meat, and wool. The stone sheep offers another favorite climbing place for kids and another perfect photo opportunity for grandparents.

The 4-H Children's Garden is not only about delight, it is about education too, although here the two are not mutually exclusive. The colorful amphi-theater and demonstration plaza holds seats for eighty-eight children and is often the site for classes and entertainment. The Garden House is next to a Kitchen Garden, complete with compost display.

The Rainbow Garden is one of the most im-portant educational displays, showing children "where in the world" we get the plants we eat. The six small theme gardens that make up the rainbow-shaped area display plants native to this country or introduced to North America by immigrants. Included are: the African-American Garden, with okra, black-eyed peas, watermelon, and geraniums; the Asian-American Garden, with Chinese cabbage, chrysanthemums, and red mustard; the Hispanic-American Garden, with Mexican black beans, corn, peppers, and tomatoes; the North American Indian Garden, with tobacco, sunflowers, and pumpkins; the Pioneer Garden, with pole beans, cabbage, let-tuce, and old-fashioned flowers. The International Garden changes each year to represent plants from a different country. In 1994 Italy was highlighted and plants such as Italian basil, Florence fennel, and tomato 'Roma' were included.

In keeping with the 4-H motto (Head, Heart, Hands, and Health), the Health for Better Living Garden includes the top ten most nutritious vege-tables (based on a list from the Department of Agri-culture.) These are broccoli, cauliflower, Brussels sprouts, asparagus, spinach, carrots, peas, lima beans, sweet potatoes, and globe artichoke.

Because more than twenty-five percent of all our pharmaceutical drugs come from plants, the Pharmacy Garden offers a child a chance to see "raw medicine." Here are plants commonly used in folk medicine, such as horehound and feverfew, as well as plants that have made a major contribution to fight-ing serious diseases; these include Madagascar peri-winkle, which is used in medicines treating leukemia.

Children learn that money just might grow on trees: the Cloth and Color Garden has displays of flax plants (used in making paper money), cotton plants (used for making t-shirts and blue jeans), and various dye plants (used for coloring fibers).

The Michigan 4-H Children's Garden is operated to best meet the needs and desires of young visitors. For example, when it was noticed that children were bringing their parents to the garden at sundown to watch the evening primrose flowers open, the garden hours were promptly extended. Now the Evening Primrose Show is one of the most popular attractions at the garden.

The popularity of the Garden was instantaneous. Although original plans only called for a small plot of ground to be made into a children's garden, Jane Taylor's enthusiasm and fund-raising skills allowed a small miracle to happen and, like Jack's beanstalk, the garden grew and grew.

How lucky we are that in this child's garden, verse after verse of laughter and happy chatter are heard in a never-ending refrain. Here that most cherished characteristic of children of all ages—a sense of imagination and awe—is nurtured until it takes root and lasts a lifetime.

Historical & Community Gardens

WESTERN EXPANSION HELD *promise for many people for many different reasons. Most were drawn by the economic opportunities presented by the land; later, industrialization played an undeniably major role in the development of the Midwest. But some people traveled to this new area for more ideological reasons. Some came because they believed that in this vast new land they would be allowed the freedom to worship as they pleased. Many religious sects made their way to the midwestern areas and settled here to create communities based on the ideals, mores and laws of their own beliefs. From the settlers of the early Shaker villages to the inhabitants of the more recently established Baha'i House of Worship, religious groups have had great influence on the people and communities of the region.*

The Shakers, or "shaking Quakers," were so named for their animated movements during worship. Under the leadership of an indomitable woman, Ann Lee, the Shakers first settled in Niskayuna, New York, outside Albany, in 1776, and later moved to establish Shaker communities elsewhere.

The Shakers eventually founded nineteen villages from Maine to Indiana; the one at Pleasant Hill, Kentucky, became the third largest.

The Shaker influence in the United States and throughout the world proved to be substantial. Shakers were hard-working, innovative, and creative individuals who grew most of the food they needed and created products to sell to pay for the things they had to buy.

Although only a few of the leaders from a Shaker village were allowed to communicate with the outside world, the Kentucky Shakers still managed to have an impact on the communities surrounding theirs. The Shakers at Pleasant Hill experimented with crossbreeding livestock, and eventually Pleasant Hill became known as a leading agricultural experimental station.

ABOVE. *Phlox* (Phlox sp.) *and a daisy* (Chrysanthemum leucanthemum), *at the Shakespeare Garden.*

OPPOSITE. *The Shakespeare Garden on the campus of Northwestern University is a beautiful sanctuary for students and visitors.*

As the Shakers were thriving in Kentucky, the Rappites, a religious sect from Würtemberg, Germany, were also seeking a place in which to practice their religious beliefs unencumbered by rules and prejudices of established churches. The Rappites believed in the imminent second coming of Christ, and every decision they made was based on this belief.

In 1814 Father George Rapp established a community at Harmony, Indiana, where 1,000 men, women, and children worked at farming and trade. The industrious Rappites became adept at many different trades, from the making of fine silks to the distilling of whiskey; they sold their products to customers as far away as New Orleans.

After ten years Father George Rapp decided to move the community. He sold the town property to another community of idealists—in this case, nonreligious—whose members held the view that universal happiness came through universal education. Once again, Harmony (or New Harmony, as it was now called) showed its influence on this growing region. Among other "firsts," the community at New Harmony had the first woman's club and the first civic dramatic club in America.

By 1840 the challenge of taming the midwestern frontier was essentially over, and the landscape of the Midwest had begun to change greatly. The decades that followed brought changes of a different sort to the people of the Midwest. The rapid growth of industrialization resulted in an explosion in the number of factories in the cities. As more people moved into urban areas, the need for public green spaces became increasingly important. By the middle of the nineteenth century, rural cemeteries, with acres of lawns and trees, were filling this need and these burial grounds actually served as tourist attractions. It was quite common for families to spend a quiet Sunday afternoon strolling through a local cemetery.

As a result of this interest, the grounds and plantings of many cemeteries became more elaborate. In 1831 the Massachusetts Horticultural Society created Mount Auburn, a rural cemetery in Boston. This beautiful cemetery was designed after the famous Parisian cemetery, Père-Lachaise. During the next few decades, Mount Auburn changed from a naturalized landscape with woods and open lawns to a more formal garden landscape with ornamental plantings. It served as a prototype for other rural burial grounds in America.

Mount Auburn inevitably influenced the design of such notable cemeteries as Cave Hill in Louisville and Lexington Cemetery in Lexington, Kentucky. Rural cemeteries played an undeniably important role in landscape architecture in this country. These peaceful, natural settings, offering large open spaces for the public to visit, were the precursors of parks and botanical gardens. Many landscape architects during the latter years of the nineteenth century earned valuable experience in designing and planting parklike cemeteries such as these two outstanding ones in Kentucky.

Nonetheless, there remained a distinct difference in philosophies, for not all people thought that cemeteries should look like formal pleasure gardens. The Reverend E. P. Humphrey, who dedicated Cave Hill Cemetery in 1848, said in his dedicatory address:

A proper taste will regulate the character of the trees and flowers, and their distribution and arrangement. It will tolerate nothing in the style of the flower garden or the pleasure ground—nothing, in short, that is inconsistent with the properties of the place. But reason and taste suggest that it should be decorated appropriately by the beautiful productions of our great Creator.

"Proper taste" for a cemetery seemed to differ from one area to another; but in spite of these differences, the popularity of rural cemeteries as a quiet place to enjoy nature indicated the need for more public landscapes.

Sun and shadow are essential elements of every Jens Jensen design. The Shakespeare Garden at Northwestern University is no exception to this principle.

Shakespeare Garden*

Evanston, Illinois

TUCKED IN AND among the trees and towers of Northwestern University, the Shakespeare Garden, created and maintained by the Garden Club of Evanston, is a place "Where wild thyme blows, Where ox-lips and nodding violet grows . . . ," as Shakespeare wrote in *A Midsummer Night's Dream.* Here the flowers that Shakespeare wrote of in his plays and sonnets take root and bloom, beckoning visitors to sit and enjoy their beauty.

In 1916 the Drama League of America, in celebration of the Shakespeare Tercentenary, encouraged people to participate in the celebration by creating an English-style garden planted with the flowers and herbs mentioned by Shakespeare. The noted midwestern landscape designer Jens Jensen became enthusiastic about the idea and created a plan for such a garden. Alice Houston, a member of both the Drama League and the newly formed Garden Club of Evanston, brought the plan to the Garden Club and proposed that the club build this garden.

The members of the club set about to make it a reality. The Garden Club approached the Board of Directors at Northwestern University with the idea, and the Board approved, suggesting an area of the campus that would suit the development of the garden.

With a place and a plan, the Shakespeare Garden project was well underway when Jensen again met with the Garden Club, detailing the problems they would encounter. First, he explained, in the three centuries since Shakespeare wrote of these flowers, horticulture and plant cultivation had changed dramatically. Second, flowers that grow in England would not necessarily withstand the harsh winters of the Chicago area.

LEFT. *This photograph, taken circa 1930, shows members of the Garden Club of Evanston caring for the garden that they had established 14 years earlier.*

OPPOSITE. *The Shakespeare Garden, tucked among the buildings and towers of Northwestern University, offers an unexpected spot of color and fragrance.*

Club members were undaunted, however, and plans for the garden continued under Jensen's guidance and genius. As one club member put it, "This garden was loved into existence."

Jensen suggested that the design should be typical of an English garden planted during the Tudor era. A list of flowers mentioned by Shakespeare was secured from Stratford-upon-Avon. It was possible, though not always easy, to obtain many of these plants. The job was made more difficult by the fact that Shakespeare did not always refer to the plants by name, and many of the common names used by Shakespeare are not used today. For example, "a purple flower . . . chequer'd with white," is thought to refer to the common wood anemone; "Lurk in the Ditch" is now called pennyroyal; and "Fairies Glove" is foxglove.

Diligent fund-raising by the garden club turned a dream into reality, and the garden was dedicated in 1930. A curved stone bench at the rear of the garden provided visitors a place to sit and talk or to read, while a bronze plaque of Shakespeare helped set just the right tone.

Jensen was well known for his large, naturalistic prairie landscapes, a style very different from the small, geometrically shaped beds needed for a formal English garden. In designing the Shakespeare Garden, Jensen showed not only his genius at design, but also his ability to diversify. The Shakespeare Garden remains Jensen's most formal design. With recent renewed interest in his work, the Shakespeare Garden in Evanston is of particular importance; in 1988, it was listed on the National Register of Historic Places for its social history and design significance.

The Shakespeare Garden is small, only covering a plot seventy feet by one hundred feet. In spite of this, the garden contains all of the elements important to a Jensen design.

In the application to the National Register of Historic Places, it was written that "By subtly combining his favorite elements of stone, the hawthorn tree, and sunlight and shadow, with those more typical of Elizabethan design tenets, [Jensen] was able to create a harmony between the natural world of the Bard's England and his beloved prairieland."

Jensen often used hawthorn trees in his designs, and the Shakespeare Garden was to be no exception to this rule. Jensen believed that this tree, with its prominent horizontal lines, was representative of the dominating horizontal planes of the prairie.

He placed two hawthorns at the entrance to the garden, using them to symbolize a border between the prairie and the garden. In addition, a double row of hawthorn hedges was planted to create a living boundary around the garden. These hawthorns planted in 1920 frame the stage upon which the garden is set.

Other characteristic Jensen design elements are also included in the garden. He was famous for the way he used sun and shade, and in the Shakespeare garden, sun-dappled stones are found on the perimeter paths, the effect created when the sun filters through the hedge. Open, sunny spaces representing the prairie were created by a central grassy area.

The double row of hawthorns, the inner row clipped at eight feet, the outer at ten feet, forms an arched walkway around the perimeter of the garden. Within this wonderful living frame, the interior of the garden is planted with eight formal beds, filled with flowers. Jensen's original design called for loose borders with tall plants gracefully arching over the lawn and paths. Roses, delphiniums, peonies, and lilies bloomed with unabashed enthusiasm.

Some, such as tansy, costmary, and peppermint, became too aggressive, upstaging plants from other areas. The Eglantine rose took root so well it grew to be sixteen feet tall, threatening to impale unsuspecting visitors with its sharp thorns before it eventually took a final curtain call.

In 1941 the beds were reworked and ivy was planted to demarcate each area. In 1961 further changes were made when Korean boxwood was planted to create symmetrical parterres filled with

OPPOSITE, TOP. The Garden was developed by the Garden Club of Evanston to celebrate the Shakespeare Tercentenary. It is planted with flowers and herbs mentioned by Shakespeare.

OPPOSITE, BOTTOM LEFT. In a nook of the Garden, thyme creeps up the pedestal of a sundial.

OPPOSITE, BOTTOM RIGHT. An exuberance of Shakespeare's flowers bloom in every shade and spill over into the hearts of all who visit.

neat, low-growing plants such as saxifrage, pinks, dwarf snapdragons, and pansies.

As the garden continued to evolve, the Garden Club turned to another expert for advice. In 1990 noted English landscape designer John Brookes suggested that the parterres be removed along with the ivy and that bricks instead be used to delineate the planting beds. He also suggested that plantings be looser and less formal so that flowers would spill into the center lawn, much as they had in Jensen's original design. In addition, the symmetrical plantings were abandoned and flowers of different hues were planted in small groups so that the eye would hop, skip, and jump down the garden path, following bits and pieces of color as they appeared, rather than anticipating one bit of color after another.

Today visitors reach the garden through a shady grove of trees, complete with graceful plantings of wildflowers; once the curtain of trees parts, however, to reveal the garden itself, sunlight floods the stage, and color and fragrance and an exuberance of flowers fill the air. Shakespeare himself might have been describing the garden when he wrote, "In emerald tufts, flowers purple, blue, and white; Like sapphire, pearl and rich embroidery."

This garden is a union of cultures and countries. Combining the inspiration of a seventeenth-century dramatist, the genius of a nineteenth-century Danish landscape designer, and the creativity and energy of a twentieth-century garden club, the unique and beautiful result, full of delightful surprises, is beloved both by the citizens of Evanston and the Northwestern University community. Arches cut in the hedge frame a vista of some of Northwestern's beautiful spired buildings, while closer at hand, butterflies and birds find refuge in this quiet spot.

The Shakespeare Garden has come to have a special place in the hearts of many people. Students come to sit and read, to perform a bit of Shakespeare, or to talk quietly with a friend. Many weddings have taken place in the garden.

"There's rue for you and here's some for me," wrote Shakespeare. We are fortunate that the Garden Club of Evanston took the lines to heart, and expanded the idea to include not only rue but also dozens of other flowers. The result is a garden full of blooms for you and for me, and the words of the Bard will live on in splendid color in this small corner of Illinois.

Old World Wisconsin*

Eagle, Wisconsin

AMONG THE ROLLING hills and prairies of the Midwest, travelers can find a bit of history snuggled into a corner of southeastern Wisconsin. Old World Wisconsin, one of the nation's largest living-history museums, covers almost 600 acres and is home to over fifty buildings that display the rich ethnic diversity of the state of Wisconsin.

The Wisconsin Territory originally reached as far west as the Dakotas and included land ripe for farming and mining. When Wisconsin achieved statehood in 1848, the population was made up of native Americans, the descendants of French voyageurs, and Cornish miners.

In the decades that followed, men and women

The Shakespeare Garden measures only 70 by 100 feet, making it one of Jensen's most compact designs.

Old World Wisconsin, in the southeastern corner of the state, is one of the nation's largest living history museums, covering over 600 acres.

from all parts of Europe, hungry for land and for the opportunities presented by this vast new frontier, found their way to Wisconsin. Immigrants came primarily from Germany, Wales, Ireland, Poland, Switzerland, and Norway. Eventually Wisconsin became home to more immigrant farmers than any other state. Though excited about the opportunities found in their new land and happy to be in America, these ethnic groups held fast to the traditions of their homelands, creating a diversity of styles and cultures within the state.

Old World Wisconsin, developed by the State Historical Society of Wisconsin, pays homage to the outstanding ethnic legacy found here. Fifty-five buildings dating from 1840 to 1915 have been restored here and placed within five distinct ethnic farmstead areas. Behind many of the houses are gardens planted according to the time period and to the ethnic cul-

ture of the families who originally lived in the houses. Thus, this living-history museum brings to life not only the homes but also the gardens that were vitally important in the everyday lives of these people.

Part of the mission at Old World Wisconsin is to use historically accurate plants at each display area. The use of heirloom and old-fashioned flowers, fruits, and vegetables creates a living collection of historic plants; the display also helps preserve the genetic makeup of each of these plants.

Old World Wisconsin is spread out over approximately three miles; although it's possible to walk from one area to the next, a tram travels the roads continually, saving visitors considerable time. The main ethnic areas include German-Polish, Norwegian, Finnish, and Danish. The Yankee area contains the Sanford house, originally built in Walworth County in 1858 by American-born settlers, and the

Crossroads Village, which portrays town life as it was in the mid-1870s. Museum docents dressed in nineteenth-century-style clothing demonstrate various crafts and trades using historic tools.

For the gardener, however, it is in the fields and gardens that the greatest interest lies, for it is in these areas that the flowers, vegetables, and field crops grown during the eighteenth and nineteenth centuries are once again brought to life. Livestock, also, is of authentic lineage and includes now-rare breeds such as Lineback and Devon cattle and Morgan-Percheron horses.

For those gardeners interested in heirloom plants, Old World Wisconsin offers a unique opportunity to see the plants of yesterday growing and blooming today. Enthusiasm for heirloom flowers and vegetables has increased dramatically over the past decade. Gardeners are not only interested in the newest culti-

vars of plants, but in the oldest as well, and educating the public about the plants that our ancestors grew is one of the goals at Old World Wisconsin.

By the turn of the century, farmers and gardeners in America were able to choose from a wide variety of plant cultivars available through the nursery trade. For example, in 1900, there were approximately two hundred varieties of beans available to farmers. Of these, less than 20 percent can be found and purchased today. Some of these old-fashioned cultivars were abandoned in favor of newer strains with improved taste or greater resistance to disease. Others were lost because they were difficult to pick or gather and were not suited to mechanized harvesting. Other strains declined because they adapted to narrow environmental ranges and were thus unsuitable for mass marketing.

Although many of the old-fashioned varieties are

The gardens at Old World Wisconsin may not be colorful display gardens, but they do offer visitors the unique opportunity of seeing heirloom plants growing and blooming today.

easy to grow, heirloom gardening is sometimes challenging, as each variety of heirloom plant must be planted far enough apart to prevent cross-pollination. Institutions such as Old World Wisconsin should be applauded for their work in helping to preserve the plant and crop diversity which is so important to the horticultural world.

The gardens here are not spectacular display gardens, but are authentic representations of settler gardens. The emphasis was on the usefulness of the plants more than on their beauty—though pleasure gardens were certainly not uncommon by the 1880s in Wisconsin. A resident of the area surrounding Freistadt, Wisconsin, described this countryside in 1881:

> The land is now mostly under an excellent state of cultivation, the county at large presenting the appearance of one vast chain of gardens, with good substantial frame and stone dwelling-houses, and, as is characteristic with the Germans, most of them have elegant yards decorated with neatly arranged walks and flower beds, while the ever famous cottonwood commands a prominent place in front of the houses.

In the German-Polish section at Old World Wisconsin, the Koepsell farm displays a farmhouse dating from 1880 and a small garden where old-fashioned vegetable species are grown. Potatoes introduced at the beginning of the nineteenth century, such as Anna Cheeka's Ozette and Isles of North Germany Early, are grown here. In addition, heirloom varieties of carrots, beets, squash, onions, turnips, cabbage, beans, and peas are also grown.

The following is a partial list compiled by the agricultural staff at Old World Wisconsin that gives both the cultivar name and the date of introduction for many vegetables thought to have been grown in various parts of Wisconsin in the late nineteenth century:

Beans	Black Turtle Soup	(1832)
	Kentucky Wonder	(before 1864)
	Dwarf Horticulture	(1825)
Cabbage	Premium Flat Dutch	(1860)
	Jersey Wakefield	(1840)
Carrots	Danvers	(before 1871)
	Scarlet Nantes	(1870)
Onion	Ebeneezer Yellow	(1844)
	Wethersfield Red	(before 1862)
	Yellow Globe	(1865)
Potatoes	Irish Cobbler	(1876)
	Bliss Triumph	(1878)
	Early Ohio	(1871)
	Isles of North Germany	(1800)

Many kinds of fruits, such as strawberries, raspberries, currants, and ground cherries were grown, as well as wild fruits and dandelions that were harvested and used to make wine.

The Schulz farm, near the Koepsell homestead, dates from 1860 and has one of the most interesting and lovely gardens found in the museum. This garden boasts many different kinds of flowers, in addition to vegetables and fruits. Flax was also grown here. After being harvested in midsummer, it was then separated and spun into continuous strands which were woven into linen for underwear, petticoats, shirts, and dresses. Interpreters in the Schulz house demonstrate both spinning and weaving techniques.

The Finnish, Norwegian, and Danish areas display similar gardens behind the houses, though each shows the strong cultural ties which make them ethnically unique.

In capturing and displaying the life-styles of early settlers, Old World Wisconsin is of importance and interest. For gardeners intrigued by heirloom plants, it is truly a treat to be able to see these plants living and thriving. The plants in our gardens today are descendants of the plants cultivated by the early settlers.

Shaker Village of Pleasant Hill

Pleasant Hill, Kentucky

IN THE ROLLING hills of Kentucky, lush fields of blue-tinted grass are intersected by stone walls from centuries past. In the midst of this land, rich with a history of tobacco and horses, lies Shaker Village of Pleasant Hill, an original Shaker community now restored and open to the public. Though the Kentucky Shakers have long since disappeared (the last Shaker sister, Mary Settles, died in 1923), their influence lives on in the beauty of their crafts and gardens and their philosophy of hard work, self-discipline, and a life dedicated to God.

The Shakers were a Protestant sect, officially the United Society of Believers in Christ's Second Appearing, formed under the leadership of Mother Ann Lee. Their popular name was derived from the term "Shaking Quakers," given to them because

Though the Kentucky Shakers have long since disappeared, their influence lives on in the beauty of their crafts and gardens.

Shaker Village of Pleasant Hill

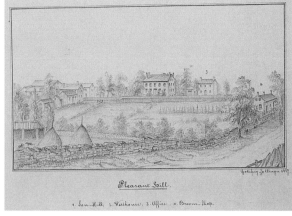

Pleasant Hill.

1. Saw Mill, 2. Warehouse, 3. Office, 4. Broom Shop.

of the trembling—a result of animated religious fervor—that often accompanied prayer. Living according to strict religious and community laws, the Shakers were well known for their diligent work habits, for using their time and effort efficiently, and for their ingenuity in creating tools and implements that enhanced this efficiency. Shaker inventions include the circular saw, a Shaker washing machine, hydraulic waterworks, a cultivator, and an apple corer and peeler.

The Shaker Village of Pleasant Hill, Kentucky, was founded in 1805 and enjoyed a surprisingly quick rate of growth. By 1823 it had a membership of 491 members and land holdings that totaled over 4,500 acres. So well regarded were the Shakers that Robert Wickliffe, a Kentucky state senator, wrote in 1831, "Let a stranger visit your country and enquire . . . for your best specimens of agriculture, mechanics and architecture, and sir, he is directed to visit the Society of Shakers at Pleasant Hill."

The Shakers were an agrarian society; an 1833 report stated, "We have between 2,000 and 3,000 acres of wheat, rye and oats. Besides our flax and 100 acres of Indian corn, broom corn and potatoes."

In addition, between 400 and 800 fruit trees were grown in extensive orchards.

The Shakers at Pleasant Hill paid close attention not only to their field crops but also to the herbs and flowers grown inside the village proper. Because laws dictated that everything in the community should have a useful purpose, no plants were grown for purely aesthetic reasons. The Sisters were even instructed to pick roses (used for their scent and flavor) without stems so that they would not be tempted to pin the flowers to their dresses or place them in a vase with water.

As the Pleasant Hill gardens increased in size and productivity, the community found that it had an excess of herbs useful for medicinal purposes. As early as 1816, members of the community began to sell these to the outside world. The Shakers are thought to have been the first commercial apothecaries in the New World. In 1820 the community had herbal remedies in the form of pills, extracts, elixirs, and powders for sale, and by 1830 business was brisk enough to require catalogs listing the various medicinal products offered. An 1851 catalog described the value the Shakers placed on their study of herbs:

"Perhaps no study contributes more to the length, utility, and pleasure of existence—which adds to the health, improves morals, tastes, and judgement more than the science of botany."

At Pleasant Hill, each communal family had its own herb garden, known as a "medical garden." Today's medical gardens were reconstructed based on notes left by Dr. John Shain, who indicated that his herb beds measured "28 by 11." The unit of measure was thought to be feet; researchers later discovered that Shain's measure had been rods (1 rod = 16½ feet). The modern result is three charming miniature representations of Dr. Shain's "medical gardens."

Within the family gardens, herbs were separated according to use: Culinary herbs were grown apart from medicinal plants, or dye plants, and so forth. From records and journal entries we know that the Shakers at Pleasant Hill either grew or gathered boneset, elder flowers, horehound, lobelia, life everlasting, catnip, thyme, tansy, sage, bugleweed, and mint. These were used to treat ailments as minor as insect bites and as serious as asthma, internal bleeding, and dysentery.

The herb industry, like the community itself, gradually died out. In 1910, the Shaker Village of Pleasant Hill had few remaining members. Celibacy and an inability to attract new members resulted in a community so small they were finally forced to end their tenure as an active religious society and the village became a simple farming community. It wasn't until 1961 that Shakertown at Pleasant Hill was formed as a nonprofit educational corporation and efforts were begun to restore the town. In 1972, Pleasant Hill was designated a National Landmark from boundary to boundary by the U.S. Department

of the Interior. The site now includes thirty-three original buildings and 2,700 of the original acres.

The gardens are small, achingly neat, and carefully labeled, all in keeping with the traditional Shaker belief in order and usefulness. But nature sometimes will not abide by the rules of men and women, and the exuberant plants break forth in an explosion of color, leaf, and fragrance. And although the gardens were not planned for aesthetics, it is impossible to ignore the beauty of these useful plants. So while almost everything in the Shaker village is lined, neat, and simple, yellow tansy spills over into the bright orange butterfly weed and spearmint simply will not stay put in its bed, but creeps and crawls and burrows underneath the ground to peek its head up in the most unexpected places. A row of lavender paints a purple portrait against the side of a stark white house, while tall spires of white valerian reach toward heaven. Comfrey grows as thickly as the tobacco in nearby fields. The garden brings a bright spot of barely controlled chaos to the austere lines of the buildings and white picket fences.

The gardens create a sense of cleanliness and usefulness. The medical garden basks in the summer sun, soaking up the heat that stimulates production of oils necessary in concocting the medicines that helped the community. Although only a small herb garden and vegetable plot are part of the grounds today, they are enough to allow the visitor to envision the extensive medicinal gardens that flourished here over a century and a half ago, when the study of botany contributed so greatly to the "length, utility, and pleasure of existence."

RIGHT. *Bright red peppers grow in the vegetable garden at Shaker Village of Pleasant Hill.*

OPPOSITE. *Shaker beliefs mandated that a plant could not be grown simply for ornamental purposes. How fortunate that the herbs grown by the Shakers, such as this lavender, were not only practical but decorative as well.*

New Harmony: What better name for a garden where the best elements of people and nature blend to create a place of peace and harmony? The history of this small southwestern Indiana town, founded by Father George Rapp, revolves around ideology. The gardens and the architecture of the town, both historical and modern, serve to illustrate the ideas and ideals of the people of New Harmony.

In 1814 the Rappites, or Harmonists, left Würtemberg, Germany, to settle in America. The group purchased 30,000 acres of land on the banks of the Wabash River and immediately set about establishing a self-sufficient town in this wilderness area. Under the leadership of Father Rapp, the group worked diligently to build the town. Their skills and labors resulted in a variety of products to trade and sell and the town prospered. From the beginning, gardening was a tradition at New Harmony. During the early days of Father Rapp and his followers, plants (particularly herbs and fruits) were grown not only for the community, but also for sale to the wider public. Records show an 1822 purchase order from Mr. George Dewey requesting plants such as grapevines, currant and gooseberry bushes, cherry, pear, quince, apple and plum trees, rose bushes, and an assortment of herbs.

After ten years, the small town was so prosperous that Father Rapp felt his followers were becoming too soft and needed a new challenge. He sold the entire town to Robert Owen, a philanthropist from Scotland, and moved the Rappites to Pennsylvania.

Owen's experiment in communal living, where education was to be the basis of all activities, was doomed to economic failure, for too many members of the community came expecting an easy life with little effort. Although the community dissolved in 1827, the impact of Robert Owen's experiment was far-reaching. New Harmony became the birthplace

Hollyhocks (Alcea sp.).

of many institutions today considered commonplace: the first kindergarten in America, the first free public-school system, the first free library, and the first woman's club.

Today Robert Owen's ideals are still bearing fruit, for New Harmony is now home to another group of people whose vision would delight both George Rapp and Robert Owen. Jane Blaffer Owen, wife of Kenneth Dale Owen, a direct descendant of Robert, has created Earthcare, a wonderful collection of gardens and a gardening resource center.

After Robert Owen's grand experiment dissolved, New Harmony experienced a gradual decline and then several decades of disrepair. It was rescued in 1941 by the efforts of people in the New Harmony community who began restoring much of the Rappites' property. The gardens at New Harmony today are found along a five-block stretch of North Street and are clustered around the Red Geranium Restaurant, the New Harmony Inn, the Earthcare Depot, and various historical buildings. They are full of unexpected surprises and range in size and personality from formal and old-fashioned to relaxed and New Age.

One of the first gardens to be restored was adjacent to a house built in 1840 (now appropriately enough called the 1840s house). Mrs. Owen restored the house and chose the outside trim to match the old-fashioned weigela which grew at the corner of the lot.

Mark Trela, horticulturist for Mrs. Owen's Red Geranium Enterprises, says that the restored garden at the 1840s house includes not only period plants but also newer varieties that added interest and color.

Nevertheless, heirloom plants are an important part of the gardens at New Harmony. Trela also took charge of restoring the garden at the Lenz House, another historic home. This time he restricted his selections to plants that the Rappites used, a list that included many herbs such as golden tansy, catmint, and sage, as well as more ornamental plants

such as peonies, daylilies, lavender, tulips, crocuses, and narcissi.

Trela admits that planting gardens only with flowers and shrubs used by the Rappites is challenging—and the most difficult part is finding seed from these older plants. He obtained many seeds from New Harmony residents whose families have gardened here for many generations.

A lush collection of hostas shaded by Bradford pear trees surrounding a circular fountain is a lovely memorial garden to Jane and Ken Owen's daughter Carol. In contrast to this garden's formality is "Ricky's Garden," a marvelous display of vegetables and flowers lovingly created by Ricky Minton, a free-spirited gardener who travels the country adopting communities and doing agricultural work. Ricky spent several months in New Harmony in 1987, double-digging

Occupying a five-block area near the Wabash River, the gardens of New Harmony reflect the community's ideals and vary greatly in size and character from old-fashioned to New Age.

the soil and designing and planting the garden. Plans for new gardens include Mrs. Owen's latest passion, a Victorian cutting garden.

The emphasis in each of these gardens is on an unqualified respect for and care of natural resources. The Earthcare Depot is a new gardening-resource center that focuses on organic gardening. In the Depot, visitors can enjoy a reading room complete with an impressive collection of gardening and horticultural books, and a small gift shop that offers books, gardening gifts, and a collection of organic seeds called Father Rapp Seeds. (Trela is quick to give credit to the Harmonists and to Robert Owen for being early environmentalists. The Rappites used the herbs from their garden for repelling insects and were meticulous about recycling and reusing everything.) The seeds are gathered from the New Harmony garden plants, which are all organically grown, and are then harvested, cleaned, and packaged by hand.

Outside the Depot, visitors are invited to examine the compost area, where half a dozen innovative compost containers are on display.

The gardens at New Harmony do not always look like a manicured botanical garden, for as Trela points out, part of educating people about environmentally sound gardening is teaching them to rethink what is beautiful. A seed can be as beautiful as a flower, says Trela, so visitors at New Harmony are allowed to see a garden in all its stages, from spring seedlings to autumn seed heads.

Learning from the decades of gardening that preceded them at New Harmony, the horticultural staff under the inspired leadership of Jane Owen has learned much of the magic and mystery of gardening. The Harmonists often planted their gardens at the front entrance to the house. It was their hope that as visitors passed through this place of beauty and peace they would leave their cares and worries behind and be refreshed as they entered the home. The gardens at New Harmony serve a similar purpose today. As the visitor passes by the hollyhocks full of richly colored blossoms and pauses to smell old-fashioned roses covering an old split-rail fence, he may easily imagine himself in a different place and century, where the idea of harmonious living was a compelling idea.

Baha'i House of Worship

Wilmette, Illinois

THE BAHA'I FAITH was founded in Persia (now Iran) during the mid-nineteenth century as an independent world religion. The guiding principles of the faith are the belief in the oneness of God, the oneness of religion, and the oneness of mankind.

The Baha'i Faith first developed in the United States in the Chicago area. By 1903, members of the faith had decided to build a house of worship there.

Although many architects submitted plans for the building, it was a French-Canadian architect, Louis Bourgeois, whose plan won unanimous approval from delegates from Baha'i communities throughout North America.

The building is a masterpiece of intricate scroll-work and design. It is nine-sided and has nine entrances, and the gardens were to be a continua-

Although all of the gardens at the Baha'i House of Worship include clipped yew hedges and Chinese junipers, each garden is different because of the variety of flowers displayed.

tion of this theme of nine, a symbol of unity of great importance to the Baha'i Faith.

It was decided that the building would be placed near the lake shore and that it have a circular area around it. From the circular area Burgeois stipulated that there "were to be nine avenues; between each a garden and in the middle of each garden, a fountain of water."

His stipulations were beautifully carried to perfection through the artistic design of Hilbert E. Dahl, a landscape architect from Louisville, Kentucky, who approached the task of designing the gardens of this holy place with a sense of great humility. Not only the design, but the plant material for the gardens, was chosen with great care. As Dahl said, "In selecting and arranging plant materials within the limita-tions imposed by Chicago climate, cognizance is taken of the need for gardenesque character possessing the richness and bounty of nature with some of the gaiety and beauty of flowers, used with caution to avoid the theatrical."

The gardens were installed during the growing season of 1952 and 1953, and represented the culmination of fifty years of fund raising, work, and dedication on the part of the members of the Baha'i Faith. The result is rows of trees and hedges softened by the addition of colorful flowers. Each garden is treated similarly, bounded by clipped yew hedges and Chinese junipers, giving a sense of unity to the entire grounds.

Through the years, each of the nine gardens has developed a different personality, yet each still retains a feeling of being a part of the whole.

BELOW LEFT. *The Baha'i House of Worship building has nine sides, each with its own entrance and garden, reflecting the group's belief in the number nine as a symbol of unity.*

BELOW. *Members of the Baha'i faith raised funds over a fifty-year period for the gardens that were installed in 1952–53.*

Seasonal plantings create color for the gardens. Every year 20,000 tulip bulbs push through the cold Illinois earth to welcome spring with opened petals. As they fade, they are replaced by summer favorites such as petunias, salvia, nicotiana, and dahlias. Fall brings plantings of chrysanthemums and other autumn favorites such as asters, colchicum, and phlox.

Many of the plants used in the gardens are included for their symbolism. For example, the roses are a reminder that life has both blossoms and thorns. Seeds are representative of growth and nurturing. The gardens, taken as a whole, represent both the variety and unity of humanity. The gardens are used to symbolize the union of the spiritual world with the everyday world. Although the nine different gardens at the Baha'i House of Worship are all slightly different, they all make up a part of the whole, and one is not complete without the others. This notion is characteristic of the Baha'i Faith. As the founder of the faith, Baha'u'llah, said, "The Earth is but one country, and mankind its citizens."

Seasonal blooms from a diversity of plants make this a lovely place to visit throughout the blooming season. Here white hydrangea welcomes summer.

Cave Hill Cemetery

Louisville, Kentucky

THE RURAL CEMETERY, or garden cemetery as it was sometimes called, was considered an American phenomenon and quickly became a point of public interest. Edmund Lee, designer of Cave Hill, said that "a place of burial may be made a delightful place of resort, and an embellishment to a town of no ordinary character, by being located in the midst of rural scenery . . ."

In May 1859, the Louisville *Daily Journal* ran an article that suggested that "there is perhaps nothing which indicates the moral character of cities as definitely as public cemeteries." If this is true, then moral character in Louisville, Kentucky, is alive and well.

Cave Hill Cemetery is not only the final resting place of many of the state's most outstanding citizens, it is also the "beautiful city of the dead," as it was often called. Today Cave Hill's reputation is far-reaching as a place of quiet beauty and as home to an unusually diverse collection of trees from around the world.

Cave Hill Cemetery, character-ized by wide expanses of lawns, lakes, and fountains, has been called the "Beautiful City of the Dead," and provides a lovely garden setting for the Louisville, Kentucky, community.

Cave Hill Farm was purchased in 1835 for the purpose of creating a rural cemetery for the thriving town of Louisville, Kentucky. It was dedicated in July 1848. By 1861 a large part of the land had been used as a Union burial ground; Confederate soldiers were buried close by. Since that time, the names of famous and not-so-famous community leaders, writers, musicians, and countless others have been etched into the grave markers at Cave Hill. Among the best known are the soldier and frontiersman George Rogers Clark, and Colonel Harland Sanders, known to millions as the founder of Kentucky Fried Chicken.

During the last century and a half, only five men have served as grounds managers at Cave Hill. The present grounds manager, Lee Squires, took over in 1974 and was faced with the challenging job of developing and maintaining a landscape that had been planted many years before. He also had to deal with the design changes instigated by his predecessors, each of whom had his own unique personality and ideas about landscaping. While one former grounds manager had planted only one kind of tree in each section, another had preferred a more naturalized approach and had planted trees at random, allowing lower branches to sweep the earth to create a shady landscape.

Squires preferred a more parklike design and trimmed the trees to create more sunlight. Doing this effectively exposed more of the markers and monuments to view and allowed more grass to grow.

While his predecessors depended on color from the trees—spring blossoms and autumn leaves—Squires has increased the amount of color in the smaller family lots by using superior hybrids and dwarf selections.

One of his greatest challenges is in maintaining the area in the present while keeping an eye toward the future. The cemetery loses fifty to sixty trees annually to disease, old age, storm damage, or root damage caused by the digging necessary for new graves. These trees are replaced with narrow, columnar trees that will not create too much shade even decades from now.

Areas that attract large numbers of visitors are planted and maintained like a garden, while less-visited sections have been allowed to mature in a more naturalistic manner. Some of the most beautiful areas include the Satterwhite Memorial, surrounded by white azaleas, and that of Charles J. Bouche, planted with a collection of sunny yellow daylilies.

Today more than 500 different species of trees and shrubs are found at Cave Hill, including a male ginkgo tree grown from seeds brought from the Far East by Henry Clay, and a yellow horn tree that grows behind the administration building.

Although Louisville has grown so that Cave Hill is no longer a truly rural cemetery—being now fairly close to the city—the cemetery is still an embellishment of "no ordinary character," and a "delightful place of resort."

Lexington Cemetery*

Lexington, Kentucky

LIKE CAVE HILL, Lexington Cemetery is much more than just a graveyard. Covering 170 acres, this beautiful park enjoys a national reputation for its beauty and tree collection. More than 200 species of trees are found here, making it an excellent place to study not only trees but also birds. A local Audubon Society chapter has identified 179 species within the cemetery.

The need for a local cemetery in Lexington, Kentucky, became acute during the cholera plagues in the nineteenth century. In 1849, twenty-five members of the community each contributed $500 to purchase Boswell's Woods, which was then made into a cemetery.

Since that time, Lexington Cemetery has remained an independent, nonprofit organization. Many well-known citizens have been buried here, including Henry Clay, Dr. Benjamin Dudley, and Coach Adolph Rupp, University of Kentucky basketball's "Winningest Coach."

Lexington Cemetery's mission is to "serve the living by honoring the dead" which it has done through its parklike areas planted with trees and gardens.

There are several separate garden areas within the cemetery. These include a sunken garden and a three-acre flower garden. Each spring 15,000 tulips and fields of spring beauties bloom at the feet of white dogwood, pink, weeping cherries and red, pink, and white crabapple trees.

These blooms gradually give way to summer flowers such as iris and hydrangeas, and annuals such as petunias, begonias, and marigolds. Fall brings a different kind of beauty as the leaves turn magnificent colors, then drop to allow the evergreens to take center stage during winter months.

The Tree Walk in the Cemetery begins at the Henry Clay Monument and has two main parts. The first loop is short, and includes the sunken garden and examples of trees such as southern magnolia, weeping cherry, yellowwood, and Osage orange. The second loop covers much more area and includes a ginkgo, cucumber tree, royal paulowina, and many kinds of oaks.

The Board of Directors of Lexington Cemetery suggests that "a cemetery is the physical manifestation of the most dignified ritual of civilization—the honoring of lives whose worth should not be forgotten." We are fortunate that the citizens of Lexington have taken such care to create this memorial that now provides peace and beauty for all visitors.

P a r k s

*BETWEEN THE 1880S and the 1920s many states and regions recognized the need
and importance to set aside large numbers of acres of natural land for public recreation.
They responded to this need by creating state and national parks, the purpose of which
was to allow easy public access to wild and natural areas. During the 1920s, several
midwestern states (particularly Indiana, Iowa, Michigan, and Wisconsin) set aside land
of notable topographical interest as state parks. Michigan, between 1919 and 1921, created twenty-three
different state parks.*

*The emphasis in selecting many of these park sites was on unusual topography, and great effort
was expended to recognize and conserve the geographic differences of many areas of the country. As
the landscape architect Henry Vincent Hubbard wrote in 1937, "I believed, and still believe, that
regional planning is based first on a recognition of the topography, the economics, the law, the political
machinery, the predispositions, and backgrounds of the people who are to be served, or more properly,
who are to be enabled to serve themselves."*

*Frederick Law Olmsted, considered the father of American landscape architecture, was untiring
in his efforts to create beautiful parks for the people. His designs include Prospect Park in Brooklyn,
Central Park in New York City, Chicago's South Side Parks, and Belle Isle and Montreal in Detroit.
Olmsted's influence was great, for his designs involved not only visual effects, but psychological ones
as well. He believed that peaceful pastoral scenes were a good antidote to stress and fatigue caused by
city life.*

*The state parks were a wonderful example of regional planning at its best, as parks used
resources available to them to meet the needs of the nearby community. While Milwaukee was building
fabulous indoor glass domes to serve its urban population, the people of Youngstown, Ohio, were*

preserving an unusually beautiful natural area close to the city. Mill Creek Park, established as a park in 1891, includes a beautiful stream, craggy cliffs, and a series of lakes; the park was further enhanced in 1958 when Elizabeth A. Fellows, an avid gardener, left land and money for the establishment of a formal garden adjacent to the park.

Many public parks were made possible by gifts and endowments from wealthy citizens. Noerenberg Gardens on Lake Minnetonka, near Minneapolis, was left to the Hennepin Parks System at the request of the Frederick Noerenberg family. Inniswood Metro Gardens, near Columbus, Ohio, was made possible through the generosity of Grace Innis, an enthusiastic gardener.

Parks not only served the public, but also became the training ground for an entire generation of landscape architects, many of whom worked with Frederick Law Olmsted, or with his son and stepson, who took over the firm after his death. Many of these young landscape architects later turned their considerable talents to designing gardens and landscapes for individuals of the Midwest as well. Together they helped sustain a sense of beauty in the heartland of America.

Yellow iris (Iris sp.).

Noerenberg Gardens

Lake Minnetonka, Minnesota

ON THE NORTH shore of Lake Minnetonka, not far from the bustling metropolis of Minneapolis, stands a small cluster of white columns in front of a beautiful formal garden complete with manicured lawns, beds spilling over with perennials and annuals, and a beautiful gazebo overlooking the lake.

The columns are all that remain of the magnificent Queen Anne style home built by Frederick Noerenberg in the 1890s. It was his wish, and that of his wife Johanna, that no one ever live in the home after the last family member died. His daughter, Lora, in compliance with this wish, directed in her will that the house be demolished soon after her own death.

Luckily, the beautiful gardens that made the Noerenberg estate such a showplace at the turn of the century were left intact, and were given to Hennepin Parks to be made into a park for the enjoyment of all. Lora Noerenberg Hoppe's will read, "I leave all of my real estate . . . to the Hennepin County Park Reserve District . . . for the purpose of establishing a memorial park in the memory of my father, Frederick C. Noerenberg, and my mother, Johanna Noerenberg, to be known as "Noerenberg Memorial County Park."

In 1860, at the age of fifteen, Frederick Noerenberg moved from Berlin, Germany, to Minnesota. Though he had neither job nor money, Frederick was full of ambition, and he and his brother took a job at a hotel in St. Paul. He soon realized that the city had many business opportunities, and he convinced a

Winding paths and colorful flower beds make Noerenberg Gardens a showplace on the banks of Lake Minnetonka.

friend in Germany to come to Minneapolis to open a brewery with him. The brewery, which eventually made Grain Belt beer, prospered, and in the early 1890s Frederick and his small family, consisting of his second wife, Johanna Sprungman Noerenberg, and their children Winnie, Lora, and Harold, built a home in the popular resort area of Lake Minnetonka.

At the end of the nineteenth century Lake Minnetonka attracted wealthy people from all parts of the country. Hotels—both grand and small—dotted the shores of the lake. Part of the popularity of the lake at this time could have been the result of an article published in 1879 by Dr. Edward Perkins, who suggested that visitors come to Lake Minnetonka for the "climatology" and for "health reasons." People came at the rate of 20,000 a year, traveling not only from many parts of the United States but from Europe as well. They arrived by rail, by carriage, and finally by streetcar.

Though many wealthy citizens from Minneapolis had summer homes on the lake, Frederick Noerenberg was one of the first to establish a year-round residence here.

The seventy-three acres that he owned included 8,490 feet of shoreline. Unfortunately, much of it had been cleared by timber companies, but Frederick, or "the Boss," as his children called him, set his mind and considerable energy and resources to beautifying the estate.

The results were stunning. Following an English style of architecture, he created an estate that included not only a large manor house with eight bedrooms, a green-tiled roof and leaded stained-glass windows, but also manicured lawns, terraced rose beds, and a working farm. At one time there were seventeen employees who took care of the house, the vegetable and flower gardens, and orchards.

Thelma Jones, in her book about the Lake Minnetonka area, wrote about Frederick Noerenberg, "The farm was his pride. It was said he could instantly spot it were a single rose missing. His house was an

TOP. *The Noerenberg family at their home, circa 1900.*

ABOVE. *This large Queen Anne–style house was one of the first permanent buildings on the shores of Lake Minnetonka. Unfortunately, the house no longer exists. The gardens were completely renovated in 1994.*

The spider flower (Cleome hasslerana), *shown here in the foreground, has a strong, sweet scent as well as a beautiful blossom.*

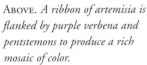

enormous Queen Anne dwelling with the usual wooden lace but magnificently built . . ."

The Noerenberg family was extremely interested in gardens and natural history. During their extensive travels throughout the world, they collected trees and plants to bring back to Minnesota. Winnie, one of the daughters, was very interested in rocks and brought several prize specimens home with her.

It was daughter Lora who showed the greatest interest in the gardens. After earning a university degree, she served as head gardener and horticulturist for the family estate. Assisting her was Ray Forde, who began working at the estate when he was a teenager and continued to do so for the next fifty-four years until he retired in 1981.

Tragically, Lora's husband was killed in an automobile accident only eighteen months after they married. They had no children and she never remarried. When she died at age eighty-five, she left the family

property and an endowment to Hennepin Parks, stipulating that the land immediately surrounding the former location of the house be used as a general public display garden, with emphasis on floral displays, and that the area north of County Road 51 be left in a natural state to be used as a wildlife refuge or sanctuary. The gardens, which cover about an acre on top of a small hillside on the lake shore, are formal with planted beds providing swaths of color next to the carefully clipped and manicured grass lawns. They were completely renovated in 1994 and are a mixture of perennials, annuals, herbs, and ornamental vegetables.

Today much of the Noerenbergs' original plant material remains in the garden. These plants include blue false indigo, queen of the prairie, dusty meadow rue, lavender mist meadow rue, Solomon's seal, monkshood, and peony. Also from the original garden is the grape arbor, a standard in many turn-of-the-century gardens. The arbor has been rebuilt twice but is still covered with the grapes planted in the Noerenbergs' time. It is a small variety, ripening later than most other grapes, and it is best suited for making jelly.

Visitors to the gardens today are greeted by a sea of pale pink and lavender. Tall sails of purple verbena bend in the breeze, while waves of ornamental grasses show crests of white from foxglove and flowering tobacco. Big, fuzzy gray green leaves of *Salvia argentina* grow close to the ground at the feet of larger, more colorful plants such as cosmos, penstemons, and foxglove.

Down by the water's edge, the original boathouse provided the Noerenbergs' visitors a place to sit and view the lake. The pagodalike roof and exposed roof supports were inspired by the Noerenbergs' trip to the Orient at the turn of the century. Today the restored building shelters visitors to the Park from sun or rain.

Though many of the wealthy families planted gardens on the shores of Lake Minnetonka, the Noerenbergs' garden was something very special, featuring more than 7,000 plants. The family not only used these for their own pleasure, but shared them with local hospitals. The family, now long gone, is still sharing their flowers, and we are the happy

recipients of this heritage. The Noerenberg Gardens are a little-known treasure tucked along the shore of the lake. Though the glass-enclosed yacht no longer exists, and the grand old house was torn down, the garden lives on, with scents and fragrances as fresh as the day they were planted by Frederick Noerenberg.

Native grasses grown among purple verbena catch the last rays of the afternoon sun, creating an incomparable display of light and shadow.

Eli Lilly Garden

Indianapolis, Indiana

THE UNION OF art and nature is an ancient one, for the beauty of the natural world has provided inspiration for artists since the time of the prehistoric cave paintings. If artists make it possible for us to enjoy the beauty of nature indoors through their

paintings, it seems natural that a museum should take art outdoors by planting beautiful landscapes. This is precisely what has happened at the Indianapolis Museum of Art, where art and nature, gardens and culture have combined to create a rich and var-

ied environment. The museum grounds have been developed into a series of gardens, some new, some historic, but all created through the eye of an artist.

The land on which the museum is located has a long and interesting history. In 1907 two officials of the Indianapolis Water Company, L. C. Boyd and Hugh McK. Landon, suggested that a large parcel of land located to the north of Indianapolis and bordered on one side by a barge canal, be developed into a residential area. Although the tract under consideration was full of deep ravines and gravel pits, the project was deemed feasible and work soon began on some of the most beautiful estates in the area.

Landon chose a site for his own home that was high on a bluff overlooking the canal. He began work on the mansion in 1908 and during the next three years, built a twenty-two-room house in the style of an eighteenth-century French chateau; he called the house Oldfields.

Once the house was completed, the Landons turned their attention to the grounds and in 1920 commissioned the renowned landscape architectural firm of Olmsted Brothers, from Brookline, Massachusetts, to design a series of gardens. Percival Gallagher, who was with the Olmsted firm, worked with the Landons for seven years to create a landscape of noteworthy beauty.

In 1932 Oldfields was purchased by Mr. and Mrs. J. K. Lilly, Jr. The Lillys made significant changes to the house, but essentially left the original Olmsted Brothers design of the grounds intact. Although the Lillys did not maintain the gardens with the same intensive care shown by the Landons, they did make significant additions to the grounds. In 1940 they expanded the original greenhouses, and on pastureland adjacent to the existing gardens built the Recreation House, now used as the Garden on the Green Restaurant, and added the Garden of the Four Seasons, designed by Anne Bruce Haldeman.

They also built a house for their son, Josiah K. Lilly, III (Joe). This new addition was appropriately called Newfields. Eventually all the family land was consolidated and in 1966 was donated by the children of J. K. Lilly, Jr., to the Art Association of Indianapolis, now known as the Indianapolis Museum of Art.

It proved to be an exciting spot for a museum building, and in 1971 construction began on the new museum. Although the grounds were already extensive, a 1972 gift of one hundred acres of land between the old barge canal and the White River provided an extensive parklike setting for the museum. The grounds now total 152 acres, including a forty-acre, man-made lake.

In 1978 the Indianapolis Museum of Art designated the grounds the Eli Lilly Botanical Garden to honor him for his generous donations to the Indianapolis Museum of Art. The original mansion was dedicated the Lilly Pavilion of Decorative Arts. One of the museum's primary goals was to retain the lovely ambiance of the former Lilly estate. Because the emphasis of the Garden is on maintaining a landscape of aesthetic beauty rather than horticultural collections, the word "Botanical" was eventually dropped from the title.

The twenty-six acres surrounding the museum buildings have been developed into a series of gardens and landscaped areas. In front of the main museum building the plaza gardens make a stunning entryway. Robert Indiana's 1970 LOVE sculpture sits on a small hill overlooking the fountain. This image, whose appeal was so widespread that it was made into a United States postage stamp, has come to symbolize the museum.

The Garden for Everyone is one of the newest garden areas at the museum. Designed to be accessible to all visitors, even those with physical disabilities, it has handrails and textured sidewalks that make movement easier for visually impaired visitors. All the beds are raised, allowing easy access to people in wheelchairs or people who cannot easily bend or stretch to reach the plants.

This garden emphasizes the senses and includes many plants with unusual scents or textures. Sweetly scented daphne and sweetshrub grow here, as do the fruity lemon balm and apple mint. Visitors are encouraged to touch the leaves of many plants, such as lamb's ears, which are thick, soft, and fuzzy.

For those who stop and listen, the sounds in this garden are also very special: water in the fountain, wind through the trees, and even an occasional bird call.

Perhaps the most beautiful of all the garden areas is the formal garden close to the Lilly Pavilion. This area features a profusion of annuals and perennials captured in the geometric beds characteristic of a formal garden. Intersecting walks divide the garden into four equal areas. Each is planted with flowers that blend and complement plants in other parts, allowing the visitor's eye to dance with delight throughout the garden. A long formal allee, bordered by woodland gardens, extends from the front of the Pavilion.

At one time the museum directors called for the removal of the original Landon greenhouse, but volunteers and members of the Museum Horticultural Society joined together to save it. Today the greenhouse is maintained through funds received from plant sales and individual donations. In an effort to better serve the community, the Horticultural Society sponsors a lecture series and classes on gardening and landscaping.

LEFT. *Statuary found throughout the grounds is a beautiful reminder of the close union of art and nature at Eli Lilly Garden. Shown here is* Sundial, Boy with Spider *by Willard Pollack.*

OPPOSITE, TOP LEFT. *Roses climb the arbor above pink dianthus at the entrance to the Formal Garden at Eli Lilly Garden.*

OPPOSITE, TOP RIGHT. *Intersecting walkways divide the Formal Garden into four equal areas. Geometric beds are filled with colors of the season.*

OPPOSITE, BOTTOM LEFT. *Purple iris, Japanese painted fern, and pink and white foxglove surround this small, graceful statue on the grounds of the Indianapolis Museum of Art.*

OPPOSITE, BOTTOM RIGHT. *This garden is a lovely combination of natural and formal areas.*

Eli Lilly Garden

Tall spires of foxglove (Digitalis sp.) *in stark white and brilliant shades of pink.*

Today Eli Lilly Garden offers a landscape of much beauty for visitors, but the promise for tomorrow is even brighter as the historical gardens of Oldfields are slowly brought to life. A master plan calls for restoration of many of the original gardens designed by the Olmsted Brothers in the 1920s. Among the most exciting of these is the ravine garden, which features many wildflowers, ferns, and native shrubs.

The restoration of this landscape is of particular importance because Oldfields is not only a rare and beautiful midwestern country estate but also a wonderful example of a place where visual and landscape arts have been united for the enjoyment of all.

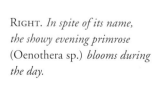

RIGHT. *In spite of its name, the showy evening primrose* (Oenothera sp.) *blooms during the day.*

OPPOSITE. *Visitors enjoy much beauty at Eli Lilly Garden now, but the future promises to be even more exciting. Eventually the original gardens designed by the Olmsted Brothers in the 1920s will be restored.*

Fellows Riverside Gardens

near Youngstown, Ohio

VISITORS TO INDUSTRIAL Youngstown, Ohio, do not expect to see remnants of wilderness such as craggy ravines and deep lakes, but that is exactly what one finds at Mill Creek Metropolitan Park, located within shouting distance of the downtown area.

This beautiful and unusual piece of property was preserved many years ago through the establishment of the Youngstown Township Park District in 1891. Nearly one hundred years later, in 1989, the name was changed to Mill Creek Metropolitan Park District, recognizing the main waterway which flows through the park.

The land within the Park located along Mill Creek was used for a variety of pioneer industries, and visitors can still find signs of these throughout the area. Lanterman's Mill was built in the early 1800s, when local residents brought wheat, corn, and buckwheat here to be ground into meal. Lanterman's is the third grist mill built at this site; today visitors can watch the old-fashioned grinding process at this restored mill. The Pioneer Pavilion, south of Lake Glacier, was once a woolen mill. Today it is a park facility open to the public.

LEFT. *Through the foresight of early conservationists, 2,530 acres were preserved in 1891 to create the Youngstown Township Park District, later known as Mills Creek Park.*

OPPOSITE. *The beauty of the park surrounds the garden. Here maroon leaves from a sourwood tree stand out against a yellow-leafed oak.*

In addition to offering views of the great natural beauty of the gorge, lakes, and streams, Mill Creek Park is also home to a cluster of the most beautiful gardens in eastern Ohio. Fellows Riverside Gardens, located at the northern tip of the 2,530-acre park, were made possible by the generosity of Mrs. Elizabeth A. Fellows, an enthusiastic gardener in the Youngstown area. When she died in 1958, she left land and money to build and maintain public gardens.

Fellows Riverside Gardens are a jewel in the heart of Mill Creek Park. The gardens beautifully display old-fashioned favorites as well as the newest, brightest, and most lovely of all the plants available to the gardener today. The gardens are composed of wide expanses of green lawn, stunning vistas, informal plantings of native plants, and formal garden areas.

A tour is best begun at the Garden Center, where a gift shop offers maps and books for purchase. Directly in front of this small, charming building is a formal garden with beds of colorful annuals lining the sides of a long rectangular lawn. At the end of the lawn is a beautiful fountain surrounded by benches and flowers that beckon the visitor to come a little closer and explore a little more. Down the steep hill toward Mill Creek are informal plantings of shade-loving species, including a host of spring-flowering bulbs that are gradually replaced by hostas and ferns during the summer months.

From the fountain, if you turn south you will be facing a long allee created by climbing roses. A magnificent flower border holds many different varieties of perennials. This area, originally planted in 1988, offers homeowners a good opportunity to see in living color which perennials thrive in this region of Ohio. At the end of this long, colorful walk is the rose garden terrace and pavilion. The view here is of Lake Glacier and the narrow gorge that surrounds it.

Elizabeth Fellows's favorite flower was said to be the rose, and Fellows Riverside Gardens is sometimes simply called "the rose garden." Climbing, miniature, historic, shrub, species, and hybrid roses have all found a home here, filling every nook

ABOVE. *The modern Rose Garden at Fellows Riverside Gardens was installed in June 1965.*

ABOVE LEFT. *A 1965 photograph shows the Fred W. Green Memorial Garden Center in Fellows Riverside Gardens.*

The Herb Garden, developed by the Mahoning Garden Club, was designed to educate people on the uses of herbs.

Summer concerts are a common event at the Victorian gazebo.

Fellows Riverside Gardens

and cranny of the garden. The greatest concentration of modern roses is found in the formal rose garden next to the pavilion. Clipped boxwood and yew hedges form the perfect backdrop for these exquisite flowers in every imaginable shade of pink, yellow, orange, red, and white.

Just outside the rose garden, nestled against the clipped hedges, the herb garden offers a nicely contrasting informality. A flagstone path weaves through plants grown for fragrance and flavoring. This area was designed by the Mahoning Garden Club for the purpose of educating people on the use of herbs; careful labeling of the plants helps accomplish this goal.

Down gracefully curving grassy paths, the rock garden displays dwarf conifers and ornamental grasses planted in and among boulders and smaller rock formations.

The view of downtown Youngstown from the Great Terrace, at the northern edge of the garden, reminds the visitor how close the urban landscape really is. It's easy to forget again, however, as you turn and face the large lawn, which is only interrupted by the Victorian gazebo and large beds full of bulbs and annuals. During spring, some 25,000 blooms herald the season. Crocuses, tulips, and daffodils burst into flower, then slowly give way to summer annuals. The tried and true petunias and marigolds are mixed with more unusual annuals that also help

Wide expanses of lawn create a canvas of green for trees and garden flowers.

OPPOSITE. *White lattice supports a multitude of climbing roses and dahlias at Fellows Riverside Gardens, while blooming annuals create a long ribbon of color.*

Fellows Riverside Gardens

Top. *Mountain laurel and hosta surround a statue of Saint Fiacre, the patron saint of gardening, at Fellows Riverside Gardens.*

Above. *A monarch butterfly sips nectar from a white milkweed.*

Opposite. *The flower beds in front of the fountain provide ideas and inspiration for gardeners who visit. New varieties as well as old favorites are grown here.*

educate the public about the variety of annual bedding plants available to the home gardener. Sometimes attractive vegetables and herbs, such as Swiss chard, with its beet-red stems, and deep green curly-leaf parsley, are planted among the flowers.

Along the edges of the Long Mall, which borders the parking lot, a succession of blooming plants offers color and interest from April to October. Trees such as magnolias and flowering crabapples provide a pretty background for smaller shrub roses and the newest selections of annuals and tulips.

Surrounding the garden is the extensive natural beauty of Mill Creek Park. It took the efforts of many people to create Fellows Riverside Gardens and to preserve not only the gardens but also the natural splendor of the park for the enjoyment of visitors today and tomorrow. A monument at the entrance to the park is a memorial to the foresight and efforts of one of these people, Volney Rogers. The words written on the memorial describe beautifully what it takes to make a dream like this come true: "Conceived in his heart and realized through his devotion."

Mitchell Park Conservatory

Milwaukee, Wisconsin

THE ONLY PLACE in Milwaukee, Wisconsin, where the grass stays green all year long is at the Mitchell Park Conservatory, affectionately called "The Domes." The conservatory is composed of three glass houses that look like giant beehives and are constructed from aluminum, glass, and steel-reinforced concrete. Each dome is 140 feet in diameter and eighty-five feet high. In other words, nearly half a football field long and as high as a seven-story building. Within these magical glass houses, flowers flourish throughout the year, cacti and succulents thrive in dry heat, and tropical rainforest plants grow luxuriously from the ground up and the roof down.

The tradition of gardening under glass was common in Europe in the eighteenth and nineteenth centuries. Although Milwaukee was settled by people from all over the world, most of the citizens were of European descent. Coming from countries where gardens and conservatories were a way of life, members of this New World community desired to continue this tradition in their adopted land.

The first parcel of land for this park was purchased in 1889 from John L. Mitchell, who later served as a U.S. Senator. By 1906 the park encompassed sixty-three and a half acres. The original conservatory was built in 1898. Although the conservatory was to be the focal point of the new park, the surrounding landscape was not forgotten. In 1904 on land adjacent to the conservatory, the Sunken Garden was planted. This garden was designed in the tradition of the European "carpet-bedding" where colorful designs were created from various foliage plants and flowers. This outdoor flower garden is still planted the same way today, and reaches its peak of beauty in late summer.

The old conservatory served the people of Milwaukee until 1955 when it was considered no longer safe for visitors. Repairing the structure proved impractical, so a design for a new conservatory was adopted and construction began in 1959. The plan called for three domes to be used as major display areas, and a fourth smaller glass house to be used as a working greenhouse. The Show Dome was completed in 1964, the Tropical Dome in 1966, and the Arid Dome in 1967. Although the structures themselves are impressive, it is the plants inside which make them truly magical.

Since its opening, the Show Dome has attracted over 10 million visitors who come to see the floral extravaganzas produced by the Parks Department. Each year five different floral shows are staged in the Show Dome: spring, summer, fall, Christmas, and winter. Each show lasts from four to seventeen weeks and has a specific historical, ethnic, or fantasy-based theme. Appropriate seasonal plants are used for each show.

The spring show is the most popular of all the Dome extravaganzas and has the greatest variety of flowers. After a long, cold winter, the people of Milwaukee are eager to surround themselves with flowers, and they come to see the show in huge numbers every year. Both Easter and Mother's Day are particularly busy times for the spring show. Over the years some of the most popular spring shows have included a Smoky Mountain spring, a New Orleans garden, a Japanese teahouse, an old rustic mill—complete with functioning waterwheel—and a Victorian garden with white gazebo.

The summer shows are usually ethnic in nature. Among others, Polynesian, Caribbean, Spanish, Italian, and Oriental themes have been used. This is the longest-running show, lasting from June to mid-September, and the flowers used in the show are replaced every three to four weeks to keep the display at the peak of perfection.

In autumn, chrysanthemums are almost always at the heart of the show. Over 100 different kinds of mums are used in the shows, which have included everything from a covered bridge to eight-foot-tall topiary birds.

On Thanksgiving Day the Dome is once again transformed, this time into an annual Christmas show that may include everything from thousands of

"The Domes," as Milwaukee citizens call the Mitchell Park Conservatory, are three glass-houses, each of which is 140 feet in diameter and 85 feet high.

poinsettias to a forty-foot Christmas tree, completely trimmed and decorated. Santa and his reindeer are frequent visitors to this winter wonderland.

The winter show is designed to chase away the cold-weather blues. Sniffles and sneezes are cured more quickly with the marvelous displays of brightly colored flowers than they possibly could be with cold pills. Pink and red azaleas form a colorful backdrop for smaller plants such as cyclamen and pansies. All are beautifully displayed in gardenlike settings, allowing the visitor to relax and stroll through a garden in the middle of winter—even if it is only for an afternoon.

Although the Show Dome is marvelously entertaining, the remaining glass domes are both beautiful to look at and educational. The Tropical Dome is

OPPOSITE. *The Show Dome boasts continuously changing display areas. Here red cannas contrast beautifully against the yellow-leafed coleus.*

filled with 1,200 different species of plants indigenous to the tropical rain forest, an area that extends over five continents on both sides of the equator. The goal in this dome is to display plants of economic importance, unusual tropical life forms, and many of the beautiful and colorful flowers found within the rain forest.

The tropics are home to many economically important plants, including beverage plants such as cocoa and coffee, woods such as teak, ebony, and mahogany, fruit trees such as avocado, and nut trees such as macadamia. Mitchell Park Conservatory is one of the few places in North America to display the curare vine, whose extract is used by certain South American Indians in making poison for blow-gun darts.

Although thousands of flower species are found in the tropics, orchids are probably the best known and most popular. The orchid collection in the Tropical Dome is impressive, consisting of over 500 species and hybrids. The American Orchid Society gave a Cultural Merit Award to one of the orchids grown here, and it now carries the cultivar name, 'Mitchell Domes'.

Epiphytes, plants that derive their moisture and nutrients from the air, and usually grow on other plants, are an important part of the tropics. In the Tropical Dome, many different kind of epiphytes can be seen. Also in this dome is one of the country's tallest trees grown under glass, a kapok tree that reached ninety-five feet before being pruned in 1989. Keen observers may spot a tiny taste of tropical wildlife, as birds and butterflies wing silently through this glass bubble, and lizards quickly slither under the nearest rock to escape curious eyes.

Moving from the Tropical Dome to the Arid Dome, visitors immediately feel as if they have entered a different world. The dampness of the tropical rain forest is gone, replaced by the dry heat of the desert. The lushness of dark green tropical plants is replaced by the thick, spiny stems of the desert plants. The Arid Dome holds one of the finest collections of desert and arid area plants in the world, consisting of cacti, succulents, shrubs, and bulbs. In this dome are plants from Madagascar, southern and eastern Africa, the Canary Islands, South America, and the deserts of North America; all are grouped according to their region of origin.

Many of the plants in the Madagascar collection were grown from seeds sent to Milwaukee by a sister garden in Madagascar. The collection is now considered one of the most noteworthy at the conservatory.

Although plants that grow in arid areas of the world can tolerate the seemingly impossible conditions of intense sun and little water in the wild, these same plants are fairly intolerant of inappropriate environmental conditions in a man-made setting. Any unscheduled fluctuation in the humidity and temperature in the Arid Dome may result in the death of these plants. Maintaining correct conditions is an art and skill which the horticultural staff at Mitchell Parks has acquired over many years. From October to March, the plants in this area are allowed to go through a natural state of dormancy. The temperature is kept at an even 50 degrees and minimum watering is done. This step results in healthier plants that bloom well in spring and summer.

The cactus collection is spectacularly beautiful when in bloom, but these are definitely plants to be

LEFT. *A pair of zebra finches enjoy the year-round warmth of the Tropical Dome.*

OPPOSITE. *A colorful display including a banana tree, fig, begonia, and caladium is found in the Tropical Dome.*

Mitchell Park Conservatory

ABOVE LEFT. *Colors and textures of the rain forest are found in the Tropical Dome, where such beautiful flowers as these orchids and bromeliads take center stage.*

ABOVE RIGHT. *Boasting more texture than color, the Arid Dome holds one of the finest collections of desert plants in the world.*

LEFT. *Bright yellow coreopsis and red geraniums are softened by tufts of ornamental grasses in the Show Dome.*

seen and not touched. Sharp spines are a trademark of these desert plants. Blooms can be found on unusual plants such as the night-blooming cereus, or on common plants such as the prickly pear.

For the citizens and visitors to the city of Milwaukee, Mitchell Park Conservatory provides a place of vibrant color and warmth during the long winter months and a place of interest and beauty all year long. But more importantly, the "Domes" allow visitors a glimpse of far-away lands. From the desert to the tropics, from history to fantasy, the Mitchell Park Conservatory is the world under glass.

Inniswood Metro Gardens

Columbus, Ohio

GRACE AND MARY Innis were two maiden ladies who created a garden of incomparable beauty in a wooded area just north of Columbus, Ohio. Mary loved the woods and natural areas and had a passionate interest in ornithology. Grace was the flower lady, and the gardens she designed and filled with plants from all over the world remain a drawing card for visitors from far and near.

The Innis sisters lived on Cleveland Avenue in Columbus for many years, and when they decided to move to the country, friends and relatives wondered if the ladies were not making a big mistake. But at Grace's insistence, in August of 1961 they moved to their new home, which they originally called Brookwood. Unwilling to abandon completely the large garden that she had cultivated on Cleveland Avenue, she arranged to have most of the plants moved to their new home in the country.

"I liked it right away," Grace said. "Of course there were a good many things about it [that] needed fixing, needed repairing, but I liked the yard, trees and the general scenery."

What Grace did with the "general scenery" earned the admiration of gardeners and horticulturists in both this country and in Europe. Although Grace seemed to love all plants and flowers, she held a special passion for daffodils, daylilies, hosta, iris, and peonies. She was not a plant breeder herself but became so well known for her skill in designing landscapes that showed off the plants to perfection, many new plant cultivars have been named after her. One, a peony, is called 'Her Grace.' Another, a hosta sport (a naturally occurring mutation) discovered in her collection, won a national hosta award for the most outstanding sport in 1986 and was registered and sold under the name 'Inniswood.' (When 'Inniswood' was first introduced to the market, the price was $200 per plant.) Daffodils have also been named for Grace and her garden, and include names such as 'Inniswood', 'Innisfree', and 'Innisberg'.

Grace's magic with plants was based on her intuitive artistic skill in modeling the garden to fit the landscape. Her success in preserving her garden for posterity in the form of the Metropolitan Park was a result of an uncompromising nature.

Grace was determined that her garden would live on, and during the last decade of her life she worked with the Metro Park system developing a master plan for the property. She remained unyielding in her expectations for what Inniswood could become, and her high standards of gardening and her reluctance to compromise sometimes made her difficult to work with. This standard of excellence, however, had an undeniable influence on the development of the park.

Prior to Grace's death in 1982, additional land was purchased to create the ninety-two-acre Metropolitan Park, whose purpose is to display a wide variety of plants that do well in central Ohio in both naturalistic and formal garden settings. Inniswood became part of Ohio's outstanding Metropolitan Park System. The boundaries of these parks are determined geographically rather than politically. Often the parks include property in more than one county.

Grace's philosophy of working with the land and creating gardens within the diverse ecosystems found on the property has been continued. A wonderful example of this is the herb garden, brought to life by the Herb Society of America, Central Ohio Unit.

After years of planning and fund-raising, the Herb Garden was completed in early 1987. Although traditional herb gardens are laid out in tight, geometric patterns, the Herb Garden at Inniswood follows curved lines and includes informal walkways and planting beds. The plants throughout the Herb Garden were chosen for their historical use in flavoring, fragrance, dye, medicine, or as ornamental plants. The entrance is marked by four vine-covered pergolas. Immediately opposite this is the Thyme Wall and the beginning of the Thyme Garden, which has many different species and cultivars of the genus *Thymus*. Here thymes are grouped according to genus and use. As low-spreading ground covers, as flavorings in cooking, as ornamental plants in the garden or as food for bees, these diverse plants have myriad uses. This collection serves as a national resource for identification and collection of the plants in the genus *Thymus*.

Visitors can enjoy the scent in the Fragrance Garden while sitting in the shade of a Victorian gazebo. Essential oils from plants in this garden have been used for centuries in making perfumes, potpourris, and soaps, and many are commercially familiar—but it's a treat to smell these products in their native form. The fountain here adds to the pleasure of the garden, making it an idyllic place to sit and read or talk with a friend.

The Bible Garden in the north end of the garden is filled with plants mentioned in the Scriptures. A small collection of these herbs is planted in a handhewn watering trough dating from the 1880s.

The remainder of the Herb Garden is made up of a knot garden, displaying intertwining plants used in a traditional geometric European garden design; a Gray Garden, which shows many plants bearing silver or gray foliage; the Medicinal Garden, where healing plants are found; and the Bee Garden, which holds a combination of annual, biennial, and perennial herbs that provide nectar for bees. Artists Jane and Joe Cooper created a clay sculpture called a bee skep or hive for this garden. This piece symbolizes the history of bee-keeping and honey production.

Close to the Herb Garden, the Woodland Rock Garden, too, is in a naturalized setting where the existing site was used to the best benefit. The garden was first planted by Grace Innis in the 1960s, but was reworked in 1991. The Rock Garden has been a source of much experimentation through the years to determine which alpine species can adapt

LEFT. *The plants cultivated in the Herb Garden at Inniswood Metro Gardens are used for flavoring, fragrance, dye, medicine, and ornamental beauty.*

OPPOSITE. *Soft waves of lavender beckon the visitor into the Herb Garden at Inniswood, where the gazebo offers a shady place to rest.*

Winding flagstone paths lead the visitor through the fragrant Herb Garden at Inniswood Metro Gardens, inviting one to learn about or to simply explore the diversity of herbs.

White and purple sedum.

The Inniswood Rose Garden was created by the Central Ohio Rose Society. This beautiful section has more than 500 plants representing 150 varieties. Dr. Robert Zollinger, a surgeon and rose enthusiast, was responsible for involving the rose society in this project during the early 1980s.

In tribute to Grace Innis's favorite flowers, special attention has been given to the Memorial Garden. Here iris, peonies, and daffodils turn the area just south of the house into a fairyland of flowers during spring. Hostas and daylilies of every hue make the Memorial Garden a spot of beauty in summer too.

More than 200,000 visitors come annually to see Mary and Grace's garden, which has grown beautifully over the years. Today Inniswood Metro Gardens provide a place to learn about plants or to sit and simply contemplate their beauty. Walking trails allow more adventuresome visitors access to some of the more remote areas of the park. The original house is now a visitor's center with a nonlending library and rooms for lectures and meetings.

Grace once said that "no one should look at horticulture as a business. Gardeners are supposed to share with one another." It is said that she never allowed anyone who admired a plant of hers to go away empty-handed. Long after her death, Grace Innis is a gardener who is still sharing, for visitors who come to her garden today are always richer for the experience.

to conditions in central Ohio. Seeds for the plants used in this garden were collected not only from the United States but from Europe as well.

In memory of Mary Innis, who loved birds and other wildlife, much of the garden has been designated a nature preserve. Wildflowers already growing on the property were labeled, and hundreds of others were planted to make this wildflower garden a spectacular sight in early spring. During spring, plants such as blue phlox, bloodroot, Dutchman's breeches, trilliums, Virginia bluebells, May-apple, and spring beauty bloom in this area. Trails, including an elevated boardwalk, wind through the area, allowing visitors a close look at the flowers.

OPPOSITE. *Yellow yarrow provides a sunny backdrop for the soft, gray spikes of lamb's ear.*

Great Estates

ALTHOUGH IT WAS agriculture that brought the first economic boom to the Midwest, it was industry and manufacturing that brought great wealth to many individuals of the region. By the end of the nineteenth century the main agricultural centers were located farther west, and states like Ohio and Michigan had become leaders in industry.

It is estimated that by 1900 160,000 people were employed in industry in the state of Michigan. It was here that W. K. Kellogg and Charles W. Post made Battle Creek the cereal capital of the world, and Henry Ford's invention helped Detroit become the center of the car industry. Farther north, Herbert Dow with his Dow Chemical Company made the small town of Midland the "chemical city."

Ohio, with native sons such as the Wright brothers and Thomas Edison, was also changing from agriculture to industry by the turn of the century. Industrial growth, coupled with the expansion of the railroad network, spurred on the establishment of many cities with a population of over 5,000.

During the early years of the twentieth century, the increase in population, much of it from immigrant workers, and the transformation from an agricultural and rural state to one of cities and industries inspired wealthy people to create quiet havens to which they could escape.

The gardens and estates built by these men and women of wealth echoed their faith and love for their country. These were men like George Booth, who believed strongly in the American Arts and Crafts Movement, and Robert McCormick, who served his country as a colonel in World War I. F. A. Seiberling, who coaxed friends and neighbors to invest in a small rubber company called Goodyear, watched as the investments multiplied 10,000 times during the next twenty-five years. Wealthy, happily married, and devoutly patriotic, Seiberling built an American estate that he named Stan Hywet.

Intense regional and national pride, and an indomitable independent spirit, was brought to life in the expansive and beautiful landscapes developed at these estates. Although European influence was

ABOVE. *Four quadrants of an herb garden boast plants used for fragrance, flavor, and medicine.*

OPPOSITE. *At Cantigny in Wheaton, Illinois, pools, statuary, long avenues of trees, and broad swaths of lawn characterize the landscape.*

seen in the English-style estate landscaping of many midwestern manors, the influence of the natural beauty of the region is pervasive. The prairie was transformed to an art form by the landscape architect Jens Jensen and became an essential element in many formal midwestern landscapes.

Jensen was a Danish immigrant who moved to Chicago in 1882. Although not formally trained, he designed gardens for some of the most prestigious and wealthy citizens of the Midwest, including Henry Ford. At his death, the New York Times called him the dean of American landscape architects.

Jensen developed what was known as the "prairie style." In 1915 Wilhelm Miller described this as ". . . an American mode of design based upon the practical needs of the middle-western people and characterized by preservation of typical western scenery, by restoration of local color, and by repetition of the horizontal line of land or sky which is the strongest feature of prairie scenery."

Warren Manning, a landscape architect who worked in Frederick Law Olmsted's firm in Brookline, Massachusetts, also believed in using "typical western scenery," and was enthusiastic if not downright adamant about using native American plants. In his work at Stan Hywet, it is known that Manning hoped the view from the west terrace would evoke the idea of the American West, where there was, in Manning's words, "unlimited possibility for individuals of vision, energy, and enterprise."

For the design of the formal walled English garden at Stan Hywet, Manning recommended Ellen Biddle Shipman, whom he considered the best "flower-garden maker" in the country. Shipman was born to a wealthy Philadelphia family who opposed her career in landscape architecture. In spite of this, she used her considerable talent and energy to design spectacular landscapes that included, among others, Longue Vue Gardens in New Orleans and Lake Shore Boulevard in Grosse Point, Michigan. Throughout her career, Shipman worked hard to teach landscape architecture to other women and to open up opportunities for women in this profession.

The grand estates of the Midwest are beautiful reminders of turn-of-the-century America when men and women of wealth and influence built houses and gardens that, although designed for private enjoyment, bring great joy to the wide public today.

Ashland*

Lexington, Kentucky

STATESMAN, ORATOR, AND three times a candidate for the presidency of the United States, Henry Clay is known as a man who wouldn't give up. This tireless congressman from Kentucky, who at one time served as Speaker of the House of Representatives, is also known for saying that he'd rather be right than be president.

Six years after they were married in 1799, Henry Clay and his bride Lucretia Hart bought the property that would eventually be known as Ashland. Clay wrote to a friend, "I am in one respect better off than Moses. He died in sight of, without reaching, the Promised Land. I occupy as good a farm as any that he would have found, if he had reached it, and it has been acquired, not by hereditary descent, but by my own labor."

In its prime Ashland encompassed over 600 acres and included the main house, ice houses, barns, gardens, walks, a stable, coach house, dovecote, and greenhouse.

Years later the Clay's great-granddaughter described life at Ashland: "These two young people, so congenial in their love for the country, were very happy planning their house, planting the grounds. The fine orchards of which we read so much, great masses of Dogwood, Red Bud, White Pine, Magnolia, live to tell the story of their hobby for collecting every variety of native tree. They laid out the flower garden. Daffodils, lilacs and sweet old damask roses still lurk in sheltered corners to show us where the garden was."

It was clear that both Henry and Lucretia loved the garden. Although Henry gardened when he

In its prime, Ashland encompassed over 600 acres, and included the main house, many outer buildings, a greenhouse, and gardens.

ABOVE. *The garden was designed in a style representative of the early nineteenth century. Today staff and volunteers use the small house as an office.*

could, most of the responsibility for the grounds lay on Lucretia's shoulders. One visitor wrote that he was amazed at Mrs. Clay's duties, as she was responsible for the orchard, dairy, greenhouses, and gardens. Correspondence between them while Henry served in Washington proves that he was very supportive of her love of gardening. He wrote in March 1840, "My dear wife: . . . . We have had three or four weeks of delightful weather. I imagine you engage in gardening, and I wish that I were with you. I still hope to be so in May."

A year later he wrote to say, "Observing a large sale of plants and flowers I put your list into the hands of the public gardener, and he has procured all of them, but one . . . The difficulty is in getting them out to you, if the river should be low at Wheeling. I shall, however, do the best I can."

In spite of the difficulties of obtaining plants, the gardens at Ashland by all accounts were wonderful. The Clays' great-granddaughter's last journal entry bears testimony to this fact. "It was a lovely old garden . . . The four large squares for vegetables were bordered with shrubs and sweet old garden flowers brought from the other part of Ashland. The purple and white lilac bushes she planted then are a glorious hedge now."

In spite of the great-granddaughter's assurance that the old shrubs and flowers would show us where the garden was, the exact location of the original garden was never determined, so when the Garden Club of Lexington decided to plant a garden at the historic home of Henry Clay in 1950, they chose a new spot. The garden was designed by Henry Kenney of Cincinnati in a style representative of the early nineteenth century. No attempt was made to use historically accurate plants; as the garden club ladies pointed out, so many beautiful plants are available to us now that were not in Clay's time, why shouldn't we take advantage of them? Just as we modernize our homes, we must also modernize our gardens.

ABOVE. *The site of the original garden at Ashland has never been determined. A new site was chosen when the Garden Club of Lexington decided to plant a garden at this historic home.*

OPPOSITE. *The garden serves as a point of solitude for some and of inspiration for others in the Lexington community.*

HOME TO KENTUCKY

FLORAL DECORATIONS TAKEN FROM MRS CLAY'S SCRAPBOOK

A pen-and-ink drawing from Lucretia Hart Clay's scrapbook.

The garden measures 180 feet long and 105 feet wide and is surrounded by a brick wall. It is laid out in a series of six brick parterres. Four parterres were planted in the first phase during the early 1950s. Holly trees were planted in the two center beds and a magnolia was placed in another. The fourth parterre was built around an existing hackberry tree. Also during this first planting stage, a yew hedge was placed along the north and west edges, and a honeysuckle hedge created along the south and east boundaries. The remaining two parterres were completed by March 1953, and the rest of the garden was planted with flowers and shrubs from the garden club members' own gardens.

The long borders along the perimeter are planted with a combination of perennials and annuals that provide color for much of the year. During summer months, ferns, lilies, and daylilies weave a graceful tapestry, while astilbes shoot forth spires of pink, red, and white and bright pink geraniums huddle beneath.

East of the walled area is a smaller garden dedicated to the growth and display of peonies. The collection is composed of Saunders hybrid peonies, many of which were originally grown in the garden of Mrs. Richard Pruett. In 1986 Mrs. Pruett's daughter gave a portion of this outstanding peony collection to the Henry Clay Estate in memory of her mother.

The roses in the Ashland garden are particularly beautiful, and are a living reminder of Henry and Lucretia Clay. Every day that he was home and the roses were in bloom, Lucretia placed a Luxembourg rose on her husband's blue willow breakfast plate, a gentle illustration of her love for him.

The garden at Ashland today serves as a place of peace and solitude for many, a spot of inspiration for others. A local preacher often comes here to write his sermons, and art students from the nearby University of Kentucky often have their classes within the walls of the garden, capturing the color and essence of the garden with paint and pen.

Along with Henry Clay's house, now a wonderful museum, the garden at Ashland gives visitors a beautiful glimpse of the life of this outstanding statesman and his wife during the early years of the nineteenth century.

Kingwood Center*

Mansfield, Ohio

KINGWOOD CENTER IS a place to delight the senses. Wide swaths of cool, green grass are edged with flowers of a thousand different hues. Herbs, bending in a light breeze, release a pungent scent. The mournful cry of a peacock is interrupted by the more cheerful chirping of songbirds attracted to the safe haven that the gardens provide.

This garden and horticultural center was the former home of Charles Kelley King, a brilliant engineer and astute businessman. Little is known of King's early life. He was born in Calais, Maine, in 1867, and attended Johns Hopkins University, but left only two months before he was to graduate, presumably to care for his family during his father's illness. He later worked in the electric trolley construction business and came to Mansfield, Ohio, in 1893. King eventually worked for Frank B. Black, founder of the Ohio Brass Company. The two enjoyed enormous business success together. King, who designed a line of overhead trolley fixtures

The planting beds in front of the mansion at Kingwood Center have always drawn visitors from far and near when the tulips bloom in spring.

offered by the Ohio Brass Company, worked his way through the ranks of the company quickly and was elected president in 1928 and chairman of the board in 1946.

Charles Kelley King married Edith May Crawford in 1896 and in 1912 they purchased the property now known as Kingwood Center. King, however, was apparently a reclusive and difficult man to live with. Although his long and intense hours at work resulted in a personal fortune, he had little time left for family or civic involvement, and he and Edith divorced in 1913.

He was married a second time in 1923 to Luise Mack. The Kings built Kingwood Hall in 1926 at the unheard-of cost of about $400,000, a sum that amazed neighbors and residents of the small town of Mansfield.

The house was designed by Clarence Mack, who, in spite of his lack of formal architectural training, created a French Provincial style house and

grounds of unusual grace and beauty. The estate, which encompassed forty-seven acres, was almost completely surrounded by trees and shrubs. A long, winding drive curved from the front gates to the brick walls that then surrounded the mansion.

The gardens on the original estate were not extensive and were mostly found close to the house. The swimming pool was built in 1920, six years before the mansion was completed. Mint was planted around the pool; mown frequently, it became a small-leaved ground cover that released a delightful fragrance whenever swimmers' feet crushed the leaves. Two bathhouses were built and were surrounded with formal gardens. The trellis between these two small houses was built from pieces of slender white pine. A small thatched-roof shelter, reminiscent of an Old World cottage, was built overlooking the sunken gardens.

In spite of the grand estate he had created, Charles Kelley King, known as C.K. or Kelley to

OPPOSITE. *Kingwood Center in Mansfield, Ohio, is the former estate of Charles Kelly King, president of the Ohio Brass Company.*

Kingwood Center

145

his closest friends, still desired to keep out of the public eye. Because he never learned to drive, he left the mansion only in a chauffeur-driven limousine. Yet it was clear that he loved the estate and was happy to share it. He often allowed his grand-nephews to host parties in the ballroom. Margaret McLean, who went to work for King as a maid in 1935, said she remembered beautiful and lavish parties, many of which were held outdoors on the south terrace.

Flowers were always an important part of life at Kingwood and the mansion was filled with floral arrangements; when house-guests were expected, King himself would check the bedrooms to be sure the flowers were perfect. During spring and summer, roses and other fresh flowers were cut in the gardens and brought indoors. During colder months, cut flowers and plants from the greenhouse were used.

Whenever King was away, he had flowers from Kingwood shipped to him, for he believed they were the most beautiful in the world.

While King was still at the height of his business career, approximately fifteen years before his death, he created the plan for Kingwood Center. Childless, he decided to leave the estate and a trust fund for its maintenance to the people of Mansfield, Ohio.

Although his first plan called for Kingwood Center to be a recreational park, King eventually decided he would rather focus on horticulture and landscape. The seeds of this vision, sown so many years ago, are bearing fruit today, for Kingwood Center with its gardens, educational programs, and horticultural library is a mecca for all who love flowers and gardens.

Since King's death in 1952 and the opening of the Center in 1953, the grounds have changed drastically. Many new gardens have been created; the swimming pool was filled in and made into a formal garden; and the tennis court was eliminated when the Terrace Garden was constructed. A nature trail was built along the perimeter of the property. Walking the woods where Charles Kelly King often rode his horse gives one a wonderful perspective of the scale of this grand old estate.

As the visitor drives onto the grounds, spectacular beds filled with the annuals or bulbs of the season greet the eye. These beds have become the trademark of Kingwood Center. In spring visitors from far and near travel to see 55,000 tulips in full bloom. As spring slowly warms to summer, the beds are transformed as a new cover of color is planted. These beds are the special charge of Charles Applegate, head gardener for Kingwood Center.

"We never know what he's going to plant," said Jerry Stites, director of the Center. "All we know is that it's going to be spectacular."

And Charles Applegate never disappoints. Although he uses many familiar summer bedding plants such as marigolds and begonias, he blends them with plants that many gardeners would never even think about using. Parsley, ornamental peppers, sweet potatoes, and Swiss chard all add a touch of the exotic to help make these annual beds something to discuss all year long.

Two small gardens displaying herbs and shade-tolerant plants are found opposite the main entrance to the mansion. It is the long, tree-lined allee, however, that catches the eye and the imagination and makes a

LEFT. *Edging Kingwood Hall, ferns, fuchsia, and impatiens combine to re-create a bit of the tropics in central Ohio.*

OPPOSITE, TOP LEFT. *Benches and a gazebo help fulfill Charles King's wish that Kingwood become a mecca for those who wish to sit and enjoy flowers.*

OPPOSITE, TOP RIGHT. *Rich, golden shades of autumn leaves overshadow the last of the summer annuals.*

OPPOSITE, BOTTOM LEFT. *Tall ornamental grasses bend gracefully in the wind, showing soft shades of purple that are displayed more vibrantly in the verbena.*

OPPOSITE, BOTTOM RIGHT. *Brilliant buds of a mountain laurel cultivar* (Kalmia latifolia) *open to softer white and pink tones.*

Kingwood Center

147

closer inspection an imperative. This avenue of trees begins at the herb gardens and leads to the Draffan Fountain at the eastern end of the estate. Closely clipped grass forms a green ribbon between the trees, and on both sides hanging baskets spill over with color from begonias and other shade-loving annuals. During spring this long, formal garden is filled with blooms of tulips, azaleas, and rhododendrons.

Parallel to the allee is the Perennial Garden, where these long-lived plants are shown to perfection. Homeowners and landscape designers flock to Kingwood during the growing season, notebook in hand, to take notes on which perennials survive and thrive in this region. Each year the first weekend in May is set aside for an annual perennial plant sale.

The Duck Pond was part of the original estate and is located at the eastern end of the Perennial Garden. It is a favorite spot for visitors of all ages. Birds and wildlife have always been important at Kingwood. When Charles King lived here it is said that he would have the birds and squirrels fed on the stone wall so he could sit in the drawing room and watch. Today the Duck Pond is home to many different species of waterfowl, with about one hundred permanent residents.

The former garage, stable, and poultry house of the estate—now the Meeting Hall, Work Shop, and Exhibit Hall—are used for much of the educational programming that has become an integral part of Kingwood Center. Kingwood Center is well known throughout the region for the many horticultural shows and plant sales hosted here; generally the Kingwood staff host between fifteen and twenty horticultural shows annually, as well as many arts and crafts shows. Classes and workshops range in subject matter from making potpourri to growing daylilies, and take place throughout the year.

The Rose Garden and the Peony Garden, located behind the lower building complex, have beautiful displays of the many varieties of these plants that grow in the central Ohio area.

Draffen Fountain forms the eastern edge of the estate. A tiny knot garden is found at the other end of the grassy allee.

OPPOSITE, TOP. *The swimming pool, built in 1920, was surrounded by mint that was mowed frequently, emitting a delightful fragrance.*

OPPOSITE, BOTTOM. *Varieties in the Rose Garden are carefully labeled, providing the visitor an opportunity for both education and inspiration.*

The Greenhouses, south of the Meeting Hall, were an important part of the original estate because they supplied fresh flowers for the mansion during the winter months as well as bedding plants for the grounds and garden. The original glasshouse was replaced in 1981, and the Orangery, built in a French Provincial architectural style, was added. Over 9,000 square feet of greenhouses hold both permanent and seasonal collections.

The Formal Garden, filled with annuals and tulips in spring, is set off beautifully by statuary and other garden ornaments. The Sunken Garden was originally planted with roses so that one could view the blossoms from above. Today the Sunken Garden, still best viewed from above, delights the eye with a kaleidoscope of pastel blossoms.

The newest garden, the Terrace Garden, is a transition between the Formal Garden and the informality of the south lawn. Covering almost two acres, the Terrace Garden opened in 1994. It is a place of movement, where nothing is static. The garden is built on two terraces, and while the overall design is in keeping with the estate style of 1920, the feeling of motion is predominant. Fountains keep the water in the garden moving constantly, while ornamental grasses undulate with the slightest breeze. A purple-leafed beech, called 'Purple Fountain', shows its true colors as the wind rustles the leaves. The feeling of motion is enhanced by the many birds and butterflies attracted to the garden. Although the area was not planted as a "wildlife" or butterfly garden, plant material was chosen carefully to supply food and shelter for the winged creatures, and feeders and water contribute to make it irresistible. For people, it is a place to sit and linger, to be still in the midst of motion.

Kingwood Center combines the best horticultural elements of the twentieth century. Joining the grace and grandeur of an old estate with the creativity of some of the best gardeners in the country today, Kingwood is truly a garden of the heartland.

Dow Gardens

Midland, Michigan

A SENSE OF playful elegance marks the grounds of the former estate of Herbert H. Dow, founder of the Dow Chemical Company. The gardens are a living reminder of this dynamic man's personality, for like him, they are innovative, creative, and at one with nature.

Herbert H. Dow learned his love of plants and gardening from his grandfather Bunnell. Captain Bunnell raised a garden full of vegetables, flowers, and fruits, and instilled within his eager young grandson not only an appreciation for all living things, but also a curiosity and inquisitiveness that would mark him for life. Herbert Dow moved from Belleville, Ontario, with his family to Cleveland, Ohio, when he was twelve, but he did not leave his curiosity behind. Always tinkering and puttering around, his first invention was an incubator for chicken eggs, the first of many inventions and patents.

Herbert Dow married Grace A. Ball in 1892 and they moved to a small home on Main Street in Midland, Michigan. Having graduated from what is now known as the Case School of Applied Science in chemical engineering, Herbert was working to develop an electrolytic process for removing bromine from brine in Midland. When he blew up a plant in Cleveland, however, his chemical career seemed on shaky ground; but he was undaunted, and four years later, in 1897, he formed the Dow Chemical Company, now one of the largest chemical companies in the world.

In 1899 the Dows built a beautiful residence at the end of Main Street. The grounds were not much to look at, but Dr. Dow immediately began planting trees, shrubs, and flowers in his back lot.

In 1900 he hired Elzie Cote as his chief gardener and the gardens quickly began to take shape. Mr. Cote said, "Dr. Dow, myself and our small group of willing helpers raised every hill on the property, dug the winding, twisting, artificial lake a half mile long, planted . . . mostly native trees and shrubs. We also planned or planted the two-hundred-odd varieties of annual and perennial flowers. This makes the whole garden artificial, but the fact is well disguised by the informality of the place, for which we owe a debt of gratitude to Mother Nature."

Although Herbert Dow seemed to love all kinds of plants, he had a special interest in fruits and fruit trees. In 1902 he wrote to a friend, "My hobby is fruit trees, and we have more than a hundred varieties in our back lot. The Japanese plums seem to be the most phenomenal trees we have. I have nearly 40 varieties of plums."

Family members recall that he was also inordinately pleased with his melon crop (grown where "the bumps" are today.) Each member of the household would have to taste and grade the melons each season to determine the sweetest ones. Seeds from these varieties were saved to be planted the following year.

Although the basic design of the garden has remained the same since Dr. Dow and Elzie Cote first began work in 1900, changes did occur in 1973 when Alden Ball Dow redesigned much of the grounds. Herbert and Grace Dow's youngest son, Alden was a well-known architect who worked under Frank Lloyd Wright. He was passionate about land and water forms blending together, a philosophy that is brought to life in the Dow Gardens.

He enlarged the ponds and added a small stream and a waterfall. The old melon patch, which had been changed into a flat lawn, he made into a series of undulating mounds, affectionately called "the bumps." Why? Just for fun.

In 1975 Alden Dow designed and added the two

red bridges that span the small stream and added a graceful white bridge, replacing an old stone bridge that his father had designed.

Many people see the red bridges and conclude that Dow is a Japanese garden. Doug Chapman, director of the gardens, is quick to point out that Dow Gardens is neither Japanese nor European, but very much an American garden. The bridges are red because the red looks good, or perhaps because red was Alden Dow's favorite color.

The main purpose of the gardens today is not only to provide beautiful displays of plant material, but also to be living proof of the range and variety of plants that thrive in central Michigan. "Right plant in the right place" is a philosophy lived every day at Dow Gardens. Plant material is chosen not because

it is familiar or trendy, but because of its beauty and ability to blend well with other plants to create a sense of a balanced plant community. Display gardens include a rose garden, herb beds, and extensive perennial and annual beds. Dow Gardens is an All-America display garden and grows the season's newest annuals to test for suitability for growth in this region.

Two of the most exciting collections in the garden are the rhododendron collection, which includes over 400 different varieties, and the crabapple collection, which features many varieties resistant to fire blight and apple scab.

The Sensory Trail was developed for physically handicapped individuals and is also used by schoolchildren, who love to feel, smell, and sometimes even taste the plants along the trail. The pool and wildflower

Top. *Stepping stones lead to one of two red bridges that span a small stream in this garden.*

Above. *White lily blossoms appear as jewels against a backdrop of green.*

Right. *Dow Gardens cover 112 planted acres and present an ever-changing landscape for visitors.*

Great Estates

A large oak tree provides shade for a bed of impatiens.

OPPOSITE. *Appearing as a spot of wilderness in Dow Gardens, this waterfall is surrounded by rich evergreen growth from Michigan conifers.*

garden are planted with some of Michigan's most beautiful native plants.

Covering 112 planted acres, Dow Gardens is an ever-changing landscape, a fact that would please its founder. The garden changes throughout the year, as one group of plants and then another comes into full, glorious bloom. New areas are being developed, new plants experimented with. Education and research are primary elements of this garden.

Elzie Cote, Dr. Dow's first gardener, once said, "Dr. Dow and I just planned our gardens the way that seemed best to us, and, as happened, our way seemed best to lots of others too." Through the years since Dr. Dow and Mr. Cote first put shovels into the ground, Dow Gardens has grown and become even more beautiful, but visitors would have to agree with Elzie Cote that their way seems best to us too.

Stan Hywet Hall and Gardens*

Akron, Ohio

JUST SOUTH OF the Ohio Turnpike near Akron, Ohio, ornate iron gates and a beautiful stone wall stand at the entrance to one of the most magnificent estates in the American Midwest. Stan Hywet Hall and Gardens was built at the turn of the century by F. A. Seiberling and his wife Gertrude, and today it remains a beautiful example of an early twentieth-century manor house and garden landscape.

F. A. Seiberling, with his brother Charles, cofounded Goodyear Tire and Rubber Company in 1898. With the increasing popularity of the automobile, the Goodyear Company enjoyed great success, and during the next decade, Seiberling accumulated great personal wealth.

The Seiberlings were very close to their six children, and when they decided to build a new home,

they wanted to create a warm and elegant place for their children, relatives, and friends. Attracted to the English Tudor style of architecture, the Seiberlings traveled to England in 1911 with their architect, Charles S. Schneider of Cleveland, Ohio, and interior decorator H. F. Huber. Here they found inspiration at such notable English manor houses as Hadden Hall and Ockwells Manor, and particularly Compton Wynyates. After visiting the latter, Frank Seiberling wrote that they were "so charmed by the picturesque beauty of Compton Wynyates that it would deeply influence the appearance of the home they were planning."

For the estate they dreamed of, the Seiberlings knew they would have to find just the right piece of property. Near Akron, Ohio, they found what

An early photograph of Stan Hywet Hall shows the west terrace, which overlooks thousands of acres of land.

Both the gardens and manor house were built in the English Tudor style.

Cool fountains, shade-giving trees, and a wide expanse of lawn make visitors feel as if they have been to the English countryside.

Stan Hywet Hall and Gardens

they were looking for—3,000 acres of farmland, orchards, and the site of an old stone quarry. It was the quarry that inspired the name for the estate; Stan Hywet comes from the Middle English words for "stone quarry."

The Seiberlings wished the landscape to match the house and envisioned the farmland as gently sloping meadows, typical of an eighteenth-century English landscape design. They were also intrigued by the site of the old stone quarry and hoped to use the steep cliffs and rocky ravines to their best advantage.

To help make these visions a reality, the Seiberlings commissioned Warren Manning as landscape architect. Manning worked with Frederick Law Olmsted and was well known for his designs, almost all of which used native American plants. By the time he began working with the Seiberlings, Manning had created noteworthy estate gardens in the East from New York to Georgia.

Even before the foundations for the house were laid, Manning started work on the landscape design. He worked closely with the architect, Charles Schneider, to site the house and create a sense of immense space and offer unusual and dramatic views to the north and west. Although many sixteenth-century English manor houses included an open courtyard within the walls of the house, Schneider and Manning decided to leave out this feature at Stan Hywet. Instead, the Great Hall opens out to the West Terrace, offering a magnificent view of the countryside. The Seiberlings were quite active, and the mansion included an indoor swimming pool, gymnasium, and bowling alley. Outdoors there were facilities for tennis, croquet, golf, swimming, skating, lawn bowling, and horseback riding.

When Stan Hywet Hall was completed, the Seiberlings celebrated with a fabulous Shakespearean Ball on June 16, 1916; family members and guests wore Elizabethan costume.

Over the years the Seiberlings were hosts to many well-known people representing government, indus-

OPPOSITE. *Warren Manning, landscape architect for Stan Hywet, was well known for his designs that included native American plants.*

ABOVE. *Rows of pink phlox are backed by white foxglove in a border in the English Walled Garden.*

try, and the arts. Visitors to Stan Hywet included four presidents of the United States, the Von Trapp Family singers, Thomas Edison, and Helen Keller.

Unfortunately, at the time of F. A. Seiberling's death in 1955, this once-magnificent American estate was in a condition of disrepair. Stan Hywet was left to the Seiberlings' heirs, who, in turn, deeded the estate to the Stan Hywet Hall Foundation, with the stipulation that the artistic and historical character of the estate be preserved. In 1972 the Foundation hired a superintendent of grounds and landscape restoration work began.

In his book *The Purpose and Practice of Landscape Architecture,* Warren Manning wrote, "The word 'garden' implies reference to a limited defined and exclusive space, and may be used in this way antithetically to the word 'landscape,' the application of which is so comprehensive that it may take in houses, lawns, gardens, orchards, meadows, mountains, and even the sky, with the stars, to the remotest nebulae."

Not surprisingly, Manning created landscapes, not just gardens, at Stan Hywet, and the result of his creative genius is still apparent today. Although the individual gardens are beautiful in their own right, it is the totality of the landscape that makes it so impressive.

As one drives into the estate, the huge expanse of lawn called the Great Meadow greets the eye. Punctuated with occasional groves of trees, this green space, reminiscent of an eighteenth-century English country estate, sets the tone and the scale for the treasures to come.

Forming the western boundary of the Great Meadow is a long allee of London plane trees, rhodo- dendrons, and azaleas. During spring this wide walk- way becomes a magic carpet as thousands of pastel petals drop from nearby flowering shrubs. The Dell, a wooded area just past the Allee, originally held a natural outdoor amphitheater. The Seiberlings' youngest daughter, Virginia, was married here.

Closer to the manor, the view is spectacular and encompasses thousands of acres of surrounding countryside. From this vantage point, it is possible to glimpse two other gardens, the walled English Garden and the Japanese Garden.

The English Garden was a favorite spot of Mrs. Seiberling, who was said to have escaped here from the stress and pressures of running a household and raising six children. In the privacy of this beautiful garden space, Gertrude Seiberling was known to write letters and occasional poetry. On the recommendation of Warren Manning, the Seiberlings commissioned Ellen Biddle Shipman to design this garden in 1929.

The focal point of the walled English Garden is a 1916 statue by Willard Paddock called "The Garden of the Water Goddess." Although the plant- ings changed greatly through the years, this garden was restored to the original Shipman design between 1990 and 1992. With its pools, fountains, and formal brick walks, it remains a graceful and charming spot for all to visit. The perennial beds, anchored by a large stone wall and balustrade below the West Terrace, display many old-fashioned flowers grown in early twentieth-century gardens. Some of these, such as the hollyhocks, phlox, and blue sage, are particularly prized. This garden is now cared for by the staff at Stan Hywet, with assistance from

LEFT. *Water and statuary form an important part of the Walled Garden, which was designed by Ellen Biddle Shipman in 1929.*

OPPOSITE. *The English Walled Garden was Mrs. Seiberling's favorite spot to escape from the stress of running a large household and raising six children.*

Above. *The Seiberlings built their estate on the site of an old stone quarry and named it "Stan Hywet," which means "stone quarry" in Middle English.*

Above right. *Pink and white phlox blooms in the Walled Garden.*

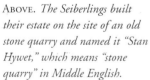

Opposite. *Although plantings in the Walled Garden have changed over the years, the garden was restored to its original design between 1990 and 1992.*

volunteers from the Akron Garden Club, which Gertrude Seiberling helped found in 1925.

The Japanese Garden, found on the hillside below the West Terrace, was an original plan of Warren Manning, although changes were made in 1974; Manning collaborated with Japanese landscape designer Mr. Otsuka when making the design. The highlight of this lush, dark green garden, located on top of an enormous cistern, is the waterfall that spills over the hillside to rocks below.

A beautiful Birch Allee connects the manor house to the stone teahouses, originally used for entertaining in the garden. The pale trunks form a natural arch, making this long pathway a very special place. Warren Manning once said that the walk along the path should be enjoyed as much as the magnificent view at the end of the allee. The black-and-white pattern on the birch trunks is repeated

on the stone path as sunshine filters through the leaves, creating playful shadows. The vista at the end of the Birch Allee overlooks the old quarry, which Manning turned into a series of lagoons that he felt gave Stan Hywet its greatest distinction.

The Cutting Garden is found on the east side of the Birch Allee. Although each individual garden adds beautiful color and a special grace to the grounds at Stan Hywet, the Cutting Garden is not only pretty but also essential to the beauty of the interior of the house, for it supplies flowers for the stunning floral arrangements that have become a trademark of Stan Hywet Hall.

In 1972 several members of the Akron Garden Club formed the Stan Hywet Flower Arrangers. "In the beginning, we came bearing flowers from our own gardens," wrote Jane DuPree, one of the original Arrangers. "We were neighbors who

Double pink impatiens snuggle in among pink splash (Hypoestes phyllostachya).

OPPOSITE. *A long allee of birches connects the manor house to the stone teahouses where the Seiberlings often entertained.*

wanted to be part of the rebirth of this sleeping estate, which had begun to stir after years of neglect. With memories of the estate in its prime, we began to make Stan Hywet appear 'lived-in' by bringing the outside in."

At first the Arrangers shared their own flowers. Eventually, a cutting garden was created in the location of the original service gardens of the estate. Once beautiful flower arrangements appeared in the manor, they became an indispensable part of the beauty of Stan Hywet Hall.

Located just outside the breakfast room is a garden planted with white, yellow, and blue flowers—the same colors used in the breakfast room itself. The Breakfast Room Garden was re-designed in 1986. Changes were made based on information from letters, drawings, and photographs from the family archives.

The formal Rose Garden, located just across the drive from the Breakfast Room Garden, provides the incomparable beauty and scent of America's favorite flower.

The motto of the Seiberling family is *"Non nobis solum"* (not for us alone). It is a motto that persists even today, for the beauty and grandeur of this great American manor house is available to all of us through the far-sighted genius and generosity of the Seiberling family. Through the years many people have collabo-rated to give this landscape a very special appeal, and today Stan Hywet blends the grace and beauty of a historical estate with the knowledge and care of peo-ple dedicated to the preservation of beauty.

Cranbrook House and Gardens*

Bloomfield Hills, Michigan

THE GARDENS OF Cranbrook House, the family estate of George G. Booth and his wife Ellen, are not only a beautiful example of turn-of-the-century landscape, they are also living proof of the influence of the Arts and Crafts Movement in America, according to whose tenets landscape design was considered to be one of the essential aesthetic arts.

George Booth was publisher of the *Detroit Evening News,* chairman of Booth newspapers, and founder of the Detroit Arts and Crafts Society. His love of art was shared by his wife, Ellen Scripps, and together they decided to create an educational community that would integrate art and religion, emphasize the importance of local craftsmanship, and make arts and crafts a part of daily life and work. Original plans for the community included a primary school, church, and art academy where artists would teach students through examples of their own work.

Booth had originally planned to include a school of landscape design and horticulture as a part of the art academy, but this part of the school was never built. Nevertheless, as the family home was completed and the Cranbrook Educational Community became a reality, the development of the surrounding landscape continued to be of great importance.

Cranbrook, named for the English village where Booth's father was born, was created on land which had been formerly used for farming. Work was begun in January 1904 to transform this worn-out land into the landscape the Booths envisioned.

OPPOSITE. *Huge heads of ornamental onion stand tall within the stone planting beds on the terrace at Cranbrook.*

BOTTOM LEFT. *Ellen Scripps Booth and Grace Booth Wallace on the north side of Cranbrook House.*

BELOW RIGHT. *An early aerial view of Cranbrook House and Gardens, showing the lake and the variety of gardens within the landscape.*

Cranbrook House and Gardens

To help him in this, George Booth hired landscape architect H. J. Corfield. Booth later wrote, "The work he [Corfield] undertook was the reclamation of a tract of land consisting of 225 acres and converting it from one of the roughest pieces of farmland possible into a country estate." The Booths, with their five children, moved into their new home in 1908.

The gardens close to the house were laid out in a formal Italian design made popular through Edith Wharton's articles on Italian villas and their gardens, serialized in *House Beautiful* in 1904.

The greatest impact on the gardens and landscape at Cranbrook came not from Corfield, but from O. C. Simonds, who worked off and on at Cranbrook from 1910 to 1923. Simonds was of the Prairie School of design and was a close follower of Jens Jensen. Simonds considered himself a "landscape gardener" rather than a "landscape architect." As he explained it, "To use the word 'architect' tends to take away that freedom and gracefulness that should go with the development of beautiful landscapes . . . A 'landscape-gardener' is one who may be thought of as trying to produce a Garden of Eden . . ."

In this respect Simonds came close to realizing his goal, for the gardens that surround the Cranbrook mansion could easily be mistaken for the Garden of Eden.

Simonds's greatest influence at Cranbrook was in allowing the plantings and architectural features to fit the contours of the land naturally and gracefully. After researching the suitability of growing various trees in this climate, Simonds decided to plant between 200 and 400 trees of each species. For the highest points, Simonds chose sugar maples, whose spectacular fall color would be easily seen from the buildings. Today there are over 100 different kinds of trees grown on the grounds at Cranbrook.

After George and Ellen Booth passed away, their youngest son, Henry, knew he needed help if he was going to save Cranbrook House and gardens. He held a huge tea party and asked everyone he knew to come and help by donating funds or volunteer hours. The result of that plea for help was the Cranbrook House and Gardens Auxiliary, formed in 1971. It is the purpose of the Auxiliary to maintain the estate for the public according to the wishes of the Booth family, a purpose they accomplish with both grace and beauty.

A tour of the estate grounds begins on a small wooded path close to the gate house. Walking through a little forest of rhododendrons, viburnum, and azaleas, the visitor comes to a point where the path splits. To the west is the Greek Theatre, to the east are the main gardens and house.

From the front courtyard of the house, visitors pass through an iron gate to the library terrace and Ellen's Garden. This area, named for Ellen Booth, is planted in her favorite colors—pinks, purples, and mauves. Here clematis and columbine, blazing star and bouncing bet, and hundreds of other flowers combine to form a pastel palette.

Across this narrow terrace is a beautiful view of the reflecting pool, originally called the Lily Pool for the number of water lilies found there. Today it is edged with annuals and perennials and a profusion of peonies. Down the steps and past the rose garden, another vista opens up. From this vantage point one can view the Bog Garden, Kingswood Lake, fields and forested areas. In spring, the meadow leading to the boathouse is covered with waves of yellow daffodils.

Beyond the boathouse is the recently renovated Oriental Garden. This garden, one of the original landscaped gardens on the property, was nearly destroyed during a 1958 flood. The story told at Cranbrook is that the spot was all but forgotten until one day in 1973, when a volunteer gardener stumbled on steps from the old garden. Work and restoration efforts have resulted in a quiet, secluded garden with water, bridges, and winding paths.

On the east side of the house, the Southern Michigan Unit of the Herb Society of America plants

and maintains both the formal herb and kitchen gardens. Just beyond these small gardens, the east terrace provides a good view of one of the most spectacular gardens on the grounds, the Sunken Garden. The fieldstone walls, dripping with ivy, form a backdrop for a carefully arranged selection of annuals and perennials.

Each year a theme is chosen for this and other gardens on the grounds, and plantings are made accordingly. One year "crazy quilts" were created from colorful annuals. Another year the theme was "ribbons," and long, slender bands of flowers made these "ribbons" come alive.

The Cranbrook Gardens, beautifully designed and planted with innovative plant material, are meticulously maintained, a huge accomplishment for even the most seasoned gardening staff. But what makes Cranbrook even more special is the fact that the gardens are designed, planted, and maintained not by paid professionals, but by a group of dedicated volunteers. This is one of the largest public gardens in the country to be maintained solely through volunteer efforts, without which the gardens at Cranbrook would not be possible. In 1994 volunteers donated almost 100,000 hours of work to the Gardens. Their love and generous spirit can be seen in every flower. For these people who give of their time so willingly, and for visitors who visit the fruits of their labor, Cranbrook stands as a reminder of the original goal of George and Ellen Booth, which was to make art and beauty a part of community life.

Cantigny*

Wheaton, Illinois

VISITORS WHO COME to Cantigny to see the beautiful and extensive gardens may be surprised to come upon a large group of army tanks sitting sedately under the trees in a fourteen-acre parklike setting. Similarly, those who come to Cantigny to see the First Division Military Museum might be just as surprised to find that the estate boasts ten acres of prize-winning gardens.

Cantigny, originally known as Red Oak Farm, was built by Joseph Medill, editor and publisher of the *Chicago Tribune.* It was inherited by his grand-son, Robert McCormick, who not only followed his grandfather in the newspaper business but also served as a colonel in the United States Army.

During World War I, Col. McCormick was the commanding officer of an artillery battalion in the First Division, now known as the Big Red One. This division launched the first American attack in

OPPOSITE. *Weeping willow droops gracefully over the lawn behind the Bur Oak Garden.*

BELOW. *Cantigny is the former home of Robert McCormick, publisher of the* Chicago Tribune *and a colonel in the army in World War I.*

May 1918. Their target was Cantigny, a small French village about fifty miles north of Paris.

McCormick inherited his grandfather's country house near Wheaton, Illinois, in the 1920s. The original house, designed as a country home by C. A. Coolidge, was a white frame dwelling with a portico of four Corinthian columns. In the 1930s McCormick and his wife Amy hired an architect from Georgia, Willis Irvin, to enlarge the house. He told Irvin, "I want the new house to last a very long time and possibly become one of the showplaces of Chicagoland because of its sheer beauty." He changed the name from Red Oaks to Cantigny.

Irvin took him at his word and remade the Medill house into a magnificent mansion. The original frame house was covered with brick, and matching wings were added. The west wing was to be used for bedrooms and sitting rooms, the east wing for the library, which McCormick liked to call the "Big Room," or sometimes simply "my room."

When McCormick died in 1955, he left Cantigny to a trust. His will read, "This trust shall continue perpetually and shall be known as 'CANTIGNY' in commemoration of the first American victory in the World War . . . My trustees, out of the income from the trust estate, shall care for, maintain and keep in good repair and condition the land and buildings and all other property pertaining thereto as a public park and museum for the recreation, instruction and welfare of the people of the State of Illinois."

Cantigny today encompasses about five hundred acres and is composed of five areas: the Visitor's Center, the Robert R. McCormick Museum, the First Division Museum, the Gardens, and the Golf Course. Approximately ten acres are planted in formal gardens, providing vistas of beauty as well as areas of study for the gardener, landscape designer, and horticulturist. One of the purposes of the gardens is to test the suitability of growth of various plants in the Illinois climate.

ABOVE LEFT: *The grounds at Cantigny are composed of many garden areas connected by wide, sweeping lawns.*

ABOVE RIGHT: *In spring, fountains are surrounded by colorful annuals, but summer brings the cooling green from trees and shrubbery.*

RIGHT. *Formal areas of the estate include this tree-lined series of terraces culminating in a small pool.*

OPPOSITE, TOP. *Robert McCormick inherited the estate from his grandfather Joseph Medill and completely renovated the house, adding matching wings to the original building.*

OPPOSITE, BOTTOM. *An early photograph of Robert McCormick's private garden at Cantigny.*

Cantigny

Twenty-one different gardens and plant collections, designed by Franz Lipp in 1967, make up the landscape here. Although each garden area is considered a separate entity, they are all connected by sweeping expanses of lawn, making this a landscape weaving of great beauty.

A tour of the gardens should begin at the visitor's center, where maps and information are available. The lawn east of the Visitor's Center is bordered by two garden areas called the Scalloped Gardens. These are planted with shade-loving annuals such as tuberous begonias, caladiums, and perennials such as astilbes. At the end of this lawn is found the Fountain Garden, which offers vistas of the Douglas-Fir Garden to the south, and the Green Garden to the north.

The Fountain Garden is most beautiful in spring, when flowering trees and shrubs transform

ABOVE. *Rows of ornamental cabbages offer an unusual variety of rounded shapes and subtle shades.*

RIGHT. *In autumn, densely filled baskets of chrysanthemums that look like colorful globes are displayed.*

OPPOSITE. *A mixed border of colorful annuals and perennials fronts a long series of vine-covered alcoves that display statuary.*

In the Bur Oak Garden, a trail
of gold through purple impatiens
and pink petunias beckons the
visitor deeper into the garden.

An ornamental cabbage in the
Bur Oak Garden.

it into a wonderland of color and fragrance. Particularly beautiful are the magnolia trees that put forth huge, fragrant blossoms. The Green Garden emphasizes the many shades of green shown by a variety of plant material. Korean boxwood, dwarf cotoneaster, winterberry, euonymous, and yews provide year-round interest, though brightly colored berries make this a very special place in fall and winter.

Just north of this area is the Bur Oak Garden. During summer months, this garden is alive with color. Thousands of annuals and perennials are planted here in wide horizontal displays of familiar and unusual plants in every color of the rainbow. Flowering vines grow vertically on lattice frameworks so that the visitor is literally surrounded by blossoms, fragrances, and color. Trees in globe and weeping shapes provide interesting focal points.

In front of the mansion, now known as the Robert R. McCormick Museum, a variety of garden areas are planted. The formal Rose Garden boasts dozens of different kinds of roses; hybrid teas, miniatures, and old-fashioned varieties. One of the most interesting roses found here is 'Chicago Peace', developed by the late Stanley Johnston.

The Idea Garden is well named, for in this small area, gardeners can find a multitude of ideas for their own home landscapes. The garden, planted in 1990, is divided into four major areas, the Children's, Vegetable, Herb, and Container gardens. In the colorful and playful Children's Garden, big building blocks are planted with flowers and vegetables, and a fish pond provides enjoyment for even the youngest visitor. Elves and topiary animals, a pizza garden, and a scientific experiment garden all serve to educate as well as entertain.

The common and unusual varieties in the Vegetable Garden are grown in conventional rows and squares as well as in more unusual plantings, such as vertical gardening, where vegetables are trained to grow on a trellis. A traditional herb garden is planted

ABOVE. *Snapdragons and impatiens.*

ABOVE LEFT. *Gently curving walks wind through beds of annuals.*

OPPOSITE. *The Bur Oak Garden holds large displays of flowers boasting every color of the rainbow. Here flowering vines climb lattice frames.*

Swaths of brightly colored flowers make Cantigny an exciting place to visit throughout the growing season.

Opposite. *The gardens at Cantigny are characterized by masses of plantings of such seasonal annuals as these chrysanthemums and salvias.*

with a large variety of herbs used for a variety of purposes from dyeing to making tea.

Gardeners who have limited space will be particularly interested in the Container Garden, where fruits, vegetables, and flowers are grown in every kind of container imaginable. Also found in this area is a waist-high garden, showing how easy it is to make a garden accessible even to those in wheelchairs.

The area south of the Fountain Garden between the Idea Garden and the Visitor's Center presents a variety of plant collections. These include a Dryland Garden, where drought-tolerant mountain and desert plants are displayed; a collection of flowering and silver foliage shrubs, including Russian olive, beauty bush, and honeysuckle; and tree collections including ornamental trees, columnar trees, and ash-dogwood, maple-viburnum, and Douglas-fir collections.

The gardeners at Cantigny seem to have adopted part of the famous motto of the First Division: "No mission too difficult." Through the years they have transformed worn-out farmland into a collection of gardens that is rich in diversity and beauty.

Arboretums

GIANT AND MAJESTIC, or frail and sweet-scented, or gnarled and twisted, trees populate the earth in myriad different forms with countless functions. Some people think of trees as just "tall plants," while others revere or even worship certain kinds. Trees are useful—bearing fruit, providing shade, and enhancing the beauty of our gardens. There are timber trees, and medicinal trees, and trees whose uses are still completely unknown. Particularly in tropical areas, many trees remain unnamed and unexplored, their potential still untapped.

Midwesterners have long acknowledged the importance of trees. In 1872 J. Sterling Morton, a member of the Nebraska State Board of Agriculture, proposed that Nebraska set aside a day to celebrate the importance of trees. The resolution passed and on April 10, 1872, Nebraskans celebrated the first Arbor Day by planting one million trees in the state. Years later his son, Joy Morton, carried out the family motto "Plant Trees" by creating The Morton Arboretum in Lisle, Illinois.

The Midwest is fortunate to have several outstanding arboretums whose common purpose is to create a living museum of woody plant materials where the public can learn and professionals can conduct research. The arboretum collections reflect different intellectual approaches, organizing trees in many different ways by plant family, such as maple, beech, or oak; by geography, such as those native to a particular state or country; or by ecosystem, such as a pine barren or an eastern wetland area. Some collections can also be based on use. At The Dawes Arboretum there is a wonderful collection of street trees, specimens which are particularly useful for urban settings. At the Minnesota Landscape Arboretum, one of the most beautiful and educational groups of plants is the hedge collection, where a variety of woody plant material has been clipped and trimmed into myriad different hedges.

Botanical research is an important part of many of these institutions. At the Minnesota Landscape Arboretum great emphasis is placed on testing and evaluating cold-hardy trees, shrubs, and ornamental plants to see if they can withstand frigid Minnesota winters. To disseminate this information as widely as possible, the Minnesota Landscape Arboretum is home to the Center for Development of Hardy Landscape Plants. The Center involves many different institutions throughout the United States and Canada whose goal is to support and encourage the breeding of landscape plants that can withstand environmental and biological stresses.

Liberty Hyde Bailey, the world-renowned botanist from Michigan, once said, "The urge to plant durable trees is man's desire for immortality, to establish something that will last far beyond his time." It is our great fortune that so many midwesterners felt this urge to plant trees. The result is a wonderful collection of arboretums that stretches from the rolling hills of Kentucky to Minnesota's North Woods.

Black-eyed Susans (Rudbeckia hirta) *showing red variations in their blossoms.*

THE MINNESOTA LANDSCAPE Arboretum is well named. An arboretum in the strictest sense—home to numerous collections of trees and woody plants—its emphasis is clearly on landscaping. The grounds boast beautiful display and demonstration gardens as well as tree specimens, and it is this union of colorful herb and flower gardens, naturalized areas, and horticultural collections that allows The Arboretum to live up to its mission to develop and disseminate knowledge of horticultural plants in Minnesota, and to provide a horticultural setting that both inspires and delights. The union of prairie and forest, highlighted by irresistibly colorful annuals and perennials, makes a visit to The Arboretum both an aesthetic and an educational treat.

The idea for an arboretum in Minnesota originated in 1956 with the Men's Garden Club of Minneapolis. At this time there was no arboretum or botanical garden in the Upper Midwest; the closest thing to it was the Excelsior Experimental Farm, originally established by the Minnesota legislature in 1878 to develop hardy apple varieties suitable for growing in Minnesota. The farm enjoyed a short success but was then closed and the land sold. In 1907 land southwest of the town of Excelsior was purchased, a new farm established, and the name changed to the University of Minnesota Fruit Breeding Farm.

Midwestern prairies hold a myriad of plants showing a marvelous abundance of color and texture.

Arboretums

A knot garden creates a formal focal point in the Herb Garden at The Arboretum.

OPPOSITE. *Each year such display beds as these featuring gray Dusty Miller and pink cockscomb are planted according to a different theme, allowing visitors to see how a garden can change from one year to the next as well as from season to season.*

Although information about fruit trees was useful and interesting, the Minneapolis metropolitan area was growing, and home gardeners became increasingly vocal in their need and desire for information about landscape plants that would thrive in this difficult climate.

The Men's Garden Club recognized this need and attempted to respond to it by growing unusual trees and shrubs in a member's backyard. Club members soon became frustrated with their lack of space, however, and turned to the Minnesota Horticultural Society for help.

Help came not only from the Horticultural Society but also from the Lake Minnetonka Garden Club, whose financial contributions made it possible to purchase 160 acres of land near the Fruit Breeding Farm. This land was turned over to the University of Minnesota, and in 1958 the Minnesota Landscape Arboretum was opened to the public.

During the next few decades, the land holdings of The Arboretum increased to 675 acres, and collections of many different types of woody plants were established. A road was cut through the acreage, providing access to the plantings.

Eventually the Landscape Arboretum and the Fruit Breeding Farm, now called the Horticultural Research Center, were combined to form a single unit of the University of Minnesota Department of Horticultural Science and Landscape Architecture. The combined acreage is now a little over 900 acres.

After leading The Arboretum through the early years and acting as director from 1958 to 1969, Dr. Leon C. Snyder was appointed full-time director of The Arboretum in 1970. Soon after this, the Leon C. Snyder Education and Research Building, including the Andersen Horticultural Library, was constructed. Perched on top of a small rise twenty miles west of the busy Minneapolis–St. Paul metropolitan area, the Snyder Building provides a view of the surrounding countryside, where the prairie meets the forest. Appearing more like a stately English manor house than a public visitor's center, this building was designed by St. Paul architect Edwin Lundie.

When Dr. Snyder retired in 1976, Dr. Francis de Vos took his place, and he made great changes at The Arboretum. He felt that small display gardens would help educate and inspire visitors, thus better fulfilling the original mission of The Arboretum. He wrote, "By presenting visitors with the wealth and beauty our earth has to offer, we hope to inspire people to strive for a more livable environment."

Under his leadership, a series of home demonstration gardens was built. These emphasize plants suitable for home landscapes in Minnesota. When Dr. de Vos retired in 1985, Peter J. Olin became the third director at The Arboretum, and the emphasis shifted to expanding research and educational programs.

Careful labeling of the plants and a wealth of educational brochures makes learning easy and fun for visitors both young and old. For those wishing to dig a little deeper, The Arboretum offers numerous classes and workshops specializing in everything from prairies to perennials, birds to bonsai, drawing to digging.

Children are given special consideration here, and in 1982 the Learning Center was constructed for the purpose of teaching youngsters about plants. Programs include botany, natural sciences, and gardening. During the academic year thousands of schoolchildren participate in programs sponsored by The Arboretum, and during the summer months, the children's garden program is full of young gardeners happily competing to see who will grow the best vegetables.

Close to the Snyder Building is the Home Demonstration Garden area, composed of nine different educational sections. The kitchen herb garden is planted with herbs most often used in cooking and flavoring, while the cutting garden displays peren-nials, annuals, and bulbs grown in easy-to-maintain rows. A rock garden has small alpine plants and dwarf shrubs planted amongst beautiful and carefully selected rocks and boulders.

One of the most popular areas is the Garden for Small Spaces, which shows home gardeners how they can best use a limited space. The Naturalistic Garden features attractive landscape plants native to Minnesota, and the Fruit and Vegetable Garden overflows with produce that grows quickly during the long summer days of the Upper Midwest.

Next to the Home Demonstration Gardens is Seisui-Tei, the Garden of Pure Water. Completed in 1985, this very special place of water, stone, and greenery was designed by Koichi Kawana. Much of the garden is symbolic. For example, the small island in the pond represents a turtle, the symbol of immortality, and pine trees, which symbolize longevity.

Leaving the Japanese Garden, the visitor enters a glade of hosta, designated the National Display Garden by the American Hosta Society. It is one of the largest hosta collections in a public garden in the world.

Just across the road and down the hill, other gardens continue to delight and inform the visitor. The Herb Garden is full of leafy green, scented plants. Enclosed by a fence, the focus of this garden is a small unclipped knot garden of gray and green santolina, germander, and lavender. Adjacent to this is the Cloister Garden, created in the style of a medieval monastery garden.

Next to the Herb Garden is the Perennial Garden, a formal area of symmetrical beds displaying perennials that produce color from late March until frost. Here the newest cultivars stand side by side with old-fashioned favorites and native plants.

The Modern Rose Garden, created in 1982, features hybrid tea, grandiflora, floribunda, miniature, and tree roses—all of which must receive special treatment to withstand the harsh Minnesota winters.

Each year the annual display gardens are planted

Appearing as beasts from a prehistoric age, conifers take on twisted and unusual shapes.

with a different theme. This variety allows visitors to see how a garden can change from one year to the next, just as it does from one season to the next. Past themes have included a Matisse painting, where the beds were planted in pastel shades of purples and pinks; an argyle sock theme, where diamond-shaped beds were filled with colorful flowers; and a patch-work-quilt theme, where the predominant colors were red and pink, and planting beds looked like huge squares of grandmother's quilt.

Almost half of The Arboretum's extensive acreage

is taken up by forested slopes and wetlands. The Three Mile Drive takes the visitor through much of this land, close to such treasures as the Old-fashioned Rose Garden, the Woodland Wildflower Garden, and the Prairie Garden. Here some of Minnesota's most beautiful native plants are displayed.

Various parking areas along the drive allow visitors the opportunity to stop and explore the many excellent tree collections. Among the most outstanding are pines, flowering crabs, shade trees, azaleas (including the Northern Lights cultivars developed at The Arboretum), hawthorns, weeping trees, lilacs, and even a collection of magnolias, surprisingly robust in this northern climate. One of the most interesting and beautiful areas is the Hedge Garden. Many varieties of evergreen and deciduous shrubs and small trees have been carefully and artfully clipped and pruned into examples of different kinds of hedges.

Labeling in the garden is impressive, but even more so is the fact that the visitor can take the information gleaned from the labels, and go to the Andersen Horticultural Library in the Snyder Building to find out where to purchase a similar plant, and how to plant and care for it. The nonlending research library is used by university students, landscape architects, gardeners, scholars, researchers, and lovers of nature.

Established with funding from Elmer L. and Eleanor J. Andersen, it now holds over 9,500 volumes and 500 periodicals. It also contains one of the largest collections of seed and nursery catalogs (both current and historic) in the country. In response to the number of people who walked in and said, "I like this plant. Where can I get it?" the library used its extensive computerized index of cultivated plants to publish the *Source List of Plants and Seeds,* which lists 47,000 different plants and 400 nurseries where plants can be purchased.

Peter Olin, director of The Arboretum, said, "I love The Arboretum, it's a place of beauty, a peaceful place where I can escape." His sentiments are shared by most people who visit here.

But The Arboretum remains more than a place of escape. It has become, through the years, a place of learning. Today The Arboretum is dedicated to fulfilling its mission of providing both education and inspiration. Through the Horticultural Research Center, the Andersen Library, the outstanding educational programming and the beauty of the gardens and collections, the Minnesota Landscape Arboretum has become a rich resource for all who love that which is green and growing.

The Dawes Arboretum*

Newark, Ohio

BEMAN AND BERTIE Dawes loved trees. They loved planting them, learning about them, and watching them grow, but most of all they loved sharing them. Through their philanthropy and their desire to share their love of the natural world, they created The Dawes Arboretum.

Born in Marietta, Ohio, Beman Dawes became interested in engineering and surveying at an early age. Years later, this interest was to result in the creation of the Pure Oil Company, and the accumulation of great personal wealth. In addition to his outstanding business career, Beman also served in Congress from 1905 to 1909.

Beman married Bertie Burr of Lincoln, Nebraska, in 1894. Bertie, a strong, independent woman, had many interests and talents including nature, gardening, fishing, and photography. She was awarded the gold life-saving medal by Congress in 1891 for personally saving two women from drowning.

In 1918 the Daweses began purchasing land for

The Dawes Arboretum, near Newark, Ohio, opened to the public in 1929, today boasts over 2,000 tree species growing on 1,149 acres.

The Dawes Arboretum

RIGHT. *Beman Gates Dawes, who began the Pure Oil Company, is shown here at a tree dedication ceremony on June 5, 1929.*

FAR RIGHT. *Bertie Burr Dawes loved fishing, nature, gardening, and photography. She is shown here dedicating an eastern white pine in 1929.*

OPPOSITE. *A quiet lake reflects early fall color at The Dawes Arboretum. A series of trails and roads allows the visitor access to many remote parts of The Arboretum.*

an arboretum whose purpose was (according to the deed of trust) to "give pleasure to the public and education to the youth; and to increase the general knowledge and love of trees and shrubs, and bring about an increase and improvement in their growth and culture."

Part of the land on which The Dawes Arboretum was founded was originally a 140-acre family farm owned by Rebecca Brumback. On the land were an 1867 farmhouse, some outbuildings, and nearby, a small cemetery containing the graves of the earliest pioneers who settled the area.

Beman and Bertie continued to acquire surrounding property until by 1929 they held about 293 acres. As soon as the Dawes acquired the land, they set about to make their vision a reality. The buildings were renovated, gardens were planted around the large house, and the farm was gradually transformed into an arboretum with the planting of an impressive collection of hundreds of different species of trees and shrubs. The land was further improved

with the creation of a large lake on the south edge and the planting of a huge hedge that spelled out the words DAWES (planted in 1932) and ARBORETUM (planted in 1942).

The Arboretum was already notable in 1929, planted with over 500 varieties of trees. It has continued to grow and prosper, and today it boasts nearly 2,000 different species growing on 1,149 acres.

One of the most exciting traditions at The Dawes Arboretum is the Tree Dedication Program, actually begun before The Arboretum was opened to the public. While the Daweses were visiting a country estate in England, Beman was much taken with a tree that had been planted when the head of the house returned from the Battle of Waterloo. Deeply impressed, Dawes felt that it would be both interesting and inspiring to invite various noted personalities to dedicate trees at his arboretum back in Ohio.

He began this program immediately and the first trees, both oaks, were dedicated by Governor James Cox and General Charles G. Dawes in June of 1927.

Since that time politicians, military leaders, sports figures, aviators, explorers, and many others have dedicated trees here. Among these are Rear Admiral Richard E. Byrd and General John Pershing, golfer Bobby Jones and Olympic athlete Jesse Owens, Orville Wright and John Glenn.

A tour of The Dawes Arboretum should begin at the Visitor's Center where there is a small nature center, a bird-watching garden, an indoor beehive, and hands-on displays. Maps and information about The Arboretum are found at the information desk. Adjacent to the center is the Bonsai Collection, considered one of the finest in the Midwest. It is particularly interesting in that most of these miniature, carefully pruned trees could live outdoors if planted in an appropriate site. Some of the oldest specimens include a ginkgo begun in 1935 and a Scotch pine begun in 1910.

The All Seasons Garden is easily viewed from the Visitor's Center. It displays perennials, annuals, and shrubs that provide year-round color suitable for the home landscape.

The extensive arboretum grounds are accessible by a series of roads and trails. The paved road covers two and one-half miles and gives an excellent overview of the tree collections and various garden areas. Additional loop roads go to the Japanese Garden (½ mile) and to the Dawes Memorial and House Museum (1 mile). Walking trails through the woods and rolling countryside provide a closer look at many of the interesting and unusual plants found here. The Holly Trail, just over a mile long, passes by the Pioneer Cemetery, Log Cabin, Holly Collection, Japanese Garden, Tall-grass Prairie, and Forest Plots.

The Japanese Garden is a beautiful, tranquil area that includes water, a bridge, and traditional Japanese plantings. It was designed by Dr. Makoto Nakamura of Kyoto University, who said that he hoped the garden would be a haven "of peace, removed as far as possible from the excitement, restlessness, and confusion of the workday world."

The Crabapple Collection forms a cloud of soft

pink, white, and red blossoms in spring and displays many commercially available cultivars suitable for the home landscape. The Maple Collection shows its best colors in fall. Some of the first trees in The Arboretum were sugar maples, planted in the north end of the property by Beman Dawes. The Maple Trail, a bit shorter than the Holly Trail, provides access to the fifty-year-old woods, the Shade Garden, and the Cypress Swamp Boardwalk.

The Shade Garden is home to many species of ferns, wildflowers, and woody plants that grow well in Ohio gardens. The Cypress Garden includes a boardwalk that juts into the swamp. Here is found one of the most northernmost stands of the southern bald-cypress tree with its characteristic "knees."

Perhaps one of the most amazing sites at The Arboretum is the gigantic hedge, trimmed to spell the words "Dawes Arboretum." The hedge is 2,048 feet (more than a third of a mile) long; each letter measures 145 feet from the base to the top. The plant material is Woodward eastern arborvitae, 'Woodwardii.' When the hedge needed replanting in 1990, over one hundred volunteers accomplished this

Bertie and Beman Dawes began purchasing land for an arboretum in 1918. Their goal was to provide a place to learn about and enjoy trees.

OPPOSITE, LEFT. *The Lacebark pine is one of many fascinating trees on the Rare Tree Walk, a one-third-mile loop trail.*

OPPOSITE, TOP RIGHT. *Pond edges provide the perfect habitat to grow such wetland favorites as cattails and iris.*

OPPOSITE, BOTTOM RIGHT. *Paper birch (Betula papyrifera).*

The Dawes Arboretum

feat in five hours. The hedge is best seen from an observation point at the southeast corner of The Arboretum property.

Just north of Dawes Lake is the Rare Tree Walk, a one-third-mile loop trail that includes some of the most unusual trees in North America. Particularly fascinating are those that show unusual bark or trunk coloration, such as the lacebark pine.

The wide expanse of rolling countryside provides a beautiful canvas for the trees and flowers that make up The Dawes Arboretum. The many plant collections, all carefully labeled, make The Arboretum a place for learning as well as enjoyment.

On the ceiling of the mausoleum where the Daweses are buried, the following verse by Henry Van Dyke is inscribed:

He that planteth a tree is the servant of God
He that provideth a kindness for many
  generations
And faces that he hath not seen shall bless him.

Bertie and Beman Dawes, by creating The Dawes Arboretum and leaving us this wonderful legacy of natural beauty, have truly provided a kindness for this generation and for many more to follow.

Bernheim Arboretum and Research Forest*

Clermont, Kentucky

A JOYOUS FEELING of wide-open spaces greets the visitor at the gates of Bernheim Arboretum and Research Forest. Long vistas of grassy meadows beckon the visitor to come in, run through the fields, and let thoughts blow in the wind like tumbleweed. As mist and clouds slowly fade in the sunshine of early morning, the silhouettes of trees appear one by one.

This feeling of peacefulness would have pleased the creator of The Arboretum, Isaac Bernheim. He felt so strongly that Bernheim Forest should be a place of peace and relaxation that he once wrote that there should be no discussion of religion or politics on the grounds.

Isaac W. Bernheim was born in the shadow of Germany's Black Forest in 1848, and he grew up just north of the place where France, Switzerland, and Germany meet. It was here, as he wandered through

the magical and sometimes mystical wilderness of the Black Forest, that Isaac developed an affinity for nature that was to remain with him a lifetime.

Bernheim did not remain in Germany. He was thrilled by stories of prosperity told by his uncle, Livingston, who had emigrated to America. When Livingston offered to lend him the money for passage and to employ him when he arrived, Isaac left Germany in the spring of 1867.

Like many immigrants, Isaac Bernheim arrived in this country with little money, and knowing only a few words of English. To make matters worse, his prospects when he arrived were grim. The United States was emerging from four years of civil war, and his uncle's factory, where he had been promised employment, was sitting idle due to lack of trade.

Luck was with him, however, for he was offered a chance to peddle "Yankee Notions"—household

Bernheim Arboretum and Research Forest serves as a living museum of both native and exotic species of trees and herbaceous plants.

Although the major emphasis is placed in trees, herbaceous plants are not forgotten. Plants such as lychnis attract not only visitors but butterflies as well.

Bernheim Arboretum and Research Forest

goods such as needles and pins, thread, socks, suspenders, and ladies' stockings—throughout a section of rural Pennsylvania. Isaac Bernheim found the open countryside much to his liking and began to prosper in his newly adopted country.

As he became more successful, he bought more goods, and a horse and wagon in which to ride. With the coming of winter, however, Bernheim realized he had put himself in a difficult situation. His horse was weak, and the wagon unfit for travel in Pennsylvania during months of snow and cold. He left his horse with a farmer friend and opened a small trading store near the town of Overton. Unfortunately, not long after this he received a letter from his friend.

Eaton March 1, 1868
Dear Sir:
I thought i would write to you and let you no your horse is dead, she dide very suddant last knite we couldant magant what was the matter of her we done all we could for her but it don no good i am very sorried for it but it cant be helpt now
G. H. Stroh

With life lacking promise in the north, Isaac Bernheim sold his remaining goods and traveled to Paducah, Kentucky, where he was employed as a clerk in a wine and spirits shop. In 1872 he and his brother Bernard acquired the business and formed Bernheim Brothers Wholesale Liquor Company.

The brothers were quite successful with their business and moved to Louisville, Kentucky, in 1888, where they continued to enjoy their prosperity.

Isaac W. and Amanda Uri Bernheim (married in 1874) were well known for their philanthropies throughout the state, but it was the creation of the Bernheim Estate, a 14,000-acre nature preserve and arboretum twenty-five miles south of Louisville that proved to be their most exciting legacy.

Isaac Bernheim was a man of vision whose dreams became a reality. He once wrote:

Dreams were mine in that far-off day in Germany, when as a boy I walked to school. They were with me when I was struggling upward in early life, when I emigrated to America, and when I tramped the country

ABOVE LEFT. *Isaac W. Bernheim, 18 years old in 1867, first worked in this country selling Yankee notions throughout rural Pennsylvania.*

ABOVE. *Through the years these first saplings planted by Isaac Bernheim circa 1930 have matured into magnificent trees.*

OPPOSITE. *Elm trees stand silhouetted against the early morning sky. Isaac Bernheim wrote that he wanted his Arboretum to be "a natural park with a profusion of things that gladden the soul and please the sight."*

Arboretums

roads of Pennsylvania selling Yankee notions from farm to farm. My dreams remained with me as my business grew and expanded through the years. They ripened into maturity at my country home in Kentucky, and in never-to-be-forgotten walks and talks with my wife.

Isaac Bernheim's dream, now called the Bernheim Arboretum and Research Forest, was begun in 1929 with the purchase of the land and the creation of the Bernheim Foundation. Through the years, Isaac had made notes as to what he wanted the forest to be:

A sanctuary for birds that fly, and fowl that find their home on water.
Foot paths and motor roads
Trees labeled carefully and protected
There shall be an arboretum for the growing of shrubs and trees
A natural park with a profusion of things that gladden the soul and please the sight.
There shall be established and maintained a nature museum.

He was also very clear as to what he did not want to happen in the Forest:

There will be no pistols, rifles or shotguns,
No trading or trafficing
No discussion of religion or politics
No distinction to be made between rich and poor, white and colored.

During his lifetime and since his death at the age of 96 in 1945, these principles have been put into action, and Bernheim Arboretum developed according to his ideas.

Today the land that makes up The Arboretum and Research Forest looks drastically different than it did when Isaac Bernheim purchased the property. In the 1920s this was worn-out farmland, stripped of beauty and nutrients. But care and effort from a dedicated staff, time, and money have allowed the land to regain much of its natural beauty, and through the unending cycles of nature, the trees are growing and the forest creatures are creeping back in, thankful for a place of refuge in

Opposite. Perennials and ground covers provide a garden-like setting in the midst of the larger natural forest areas.

Below left. Hosta is one of many shade-loving plants found in The Arboretum.

Below right. Beautyberry bush (Callicarpa japonica).

the East, where large areas of natural lands are few and far between.

Only 2,000 of the entire 14,000 acres are developed and open to the public. The remainder of the property has been left in a natural state and is used as a research site by many Kentucky colleges and universities. Entry into this area is restricted, even foot travel, for much of this research deals with observing the delicate balance of this ecosystem, which includes not only plants but also wildlife such as deer, wild turkey, and other birds.

Researchers have reestablished some areas as wildlife food plots. They also created open grassland and prairie spaces, developed watering holes, and revitalized natural salt licks to encourage the reestablishment of original plant and animal species within the property. Visitors may catch a glimpse of a new resident, the coyote, which rarely comes this far east. Speculation is that the coyote may have come from western areas when the Mississippi River froze in the winter of 1973. Approximately 216 different species of birds have been identified at Bernheim; these include game birds such as grouse, quail, and wild turkey. Numerous boxes bring many bluebirds to the forest in spring.

Although the wildlife is exciting, it is the world of plants that remains the true draw of the Bernheim Arboretum and Research Forest. Over 1,800 labeled trees, shrubs, and plants are found here in the 250 acres that have been developed into a world-class arboretum.

Particularly exciting is the Holly Collection, the largest of its kind in the United States. It includes 700 holly trees, 237 of which are American hollies. A new cultivar, 'Marilyn', was recently developed at Bernheim.

Other collections include nut trees, beech, ginkgo, oak, horse-chestnut and buckeye, crabapple and maple.

Although the Research Forest is closed to hikers, nine trails and three fire roads in The Arboretum provide for twenty miles of roads and paths for hiking through various ecosystems that include meadows as well as "deep" forested areas.

From the Nature Center it is possible to take a self-guided nature walk. Although no swimming or boating is permitted in the lakes within the Forest, fishing is allowed from the banks of Lake Nevin Monday through Saturday. Various picnic areas make The Arboretum the perfect place to spend a long spring afternoon.

Isaac W. Bernheim had a dream and the resources to make it a reality. In a letter to the trustees that he wrote in August 1939, he said that the land he had left was

to be developed and forever maintained as a center of friendly intercourse for the people of Kentucky and their friends, as a place to further their love of the beautiful in nature and in art, and in kindred cultural subjects, and for educational purposes and as a means of strengthening their love and devotion to their state and country.

The goals of the Bernheim Estate remain similar to those sketched out by Isaac Bernheim. Today Bernheim Forest serves as a living museum of native and exotic plants, allowing visitors to come and learn as well as to sit and enjoy the quiet solitude offered by a cathedral of trees.

LEFT. *St.-John's-wort* (Hypericum sp.).

OPPOSITE. *Only 2,000 of the 14,000 acres making up Bernheim Arboretum and Research Forest are developed and open to the public. The remainder have been left in a natural state.*

NOT FAR FROM the bustle of Cleveland, Ohio, down a winding country road, The Holden Arboretum provides a swath of cool green created from a forest of trees. Pale pastel hues from wildflowers and flowering shrubs color this forest in spring, making it a magical time to visit the woods, while autumn brings more vibrant hues from millions of leaves turning red, bronze, and gold. This arboretum covers 3,100 acres and was the gift of Albert Fairchild Holden, son of Liberty E. Holden, one of the founders of the Cleveland newspaper, *The Plain Dealer*.

Even though he only lived to be forty-six years old, Albert Fairchild Holden achieved meteoric success and economic prosperity as an engineer and

Bright fall colors are found not only in the changing leaves of trees but also in the golden-brown blades of grass.

The mission of The Holden Arboretum includes providing stewardship of the land, a quality experience for the visitor, and continued scientific research.

attained the position of president of the Island Creek Coal Company, and managing director of the United States Smelting, Mining and Refining Company and the American Zinc, Lead and Smelting Company. Throughout his career, Holden collected minerals and gems that he bequeathed to the Mineralogical and Geological Museums at Harvard University.

Several events brought tragedy to Holden's life. His wife, Katharine Davis, died six years after they were married, and his daughter, Elizabeth Davis, died at the age of twelve.

It was after the death of his daughter that Albert Holden began thinking of creating the Elizabeth Davis Holden Memorial Fund, the proceeds of which were to go toward building an arboretum in memory of his daughter.

Although two other locations were considered for the site of The Arboretum, in 1931 an agreement was approved to establish The Holden Arboretum on one hundred acres of land east of the city of Cleve-

land. The Holden Trust was established to provide funds for Albert Holden's two daughters, Emery May and Katharine Davis. Funds for The Arboretum were to be available only after their deaths.

The two women took an early and active interest in the new Arboretum founded by their father, and they made many generous contributions throughout their lives. However, the bulk of the funds for The Arboretum were not available until Emery May and Katharine passed away in the mid-1980s, seventy-five years after The Arboretum Trust was established.

The mission statement at Holden asserts that The Arboretum is to "promote the knowledge and appreciation of plants for personal enjoyment, inspiration and recreation; for scientific research; and for educational and aesthetic purposes."

These goals are being met today through beautiful botanical displays as well as educational programming. A new horticulture science center, devoted to research in plant breeding, was dedicated

In addition to many garden-like displays, Holden also has 20 miles of trails that wind through natural areas.

Opposite: *A dry, rocky stream bed provides a home for ornamental grasses and native plants.*

in 1994. The Holden Arboretum today boasts over twenty miles of trails, natural areas, numerous lakes, a display garden, a wildflower garden, and plant collections representing crabapples, lilacs, rhododendrons, and viburnums.

The main display garden was originally planted in the early 1940s and consisted primarily of rhododendrons, crabapples, and lilacs. The Hedge Garden, added in 1968, was the first landscaped garden in The Arboretum. Today the Main Display Garden is colored by early spring bulbs, summer annuals and autumn foliage.

An interpretive area called Sugarbush explains the art and science of making maple syrup. During early spring (when nighttime temperatures fall below 32°F and daytime temperatures still climb above freezing) pressure in the tree roots causes the sap to rise. The Holden Arboretum became involved in maple syrup research in 1978 and today maple syrup

time in The Arboretum draws thousands of visitors. The Arboretum collects about two thousand buckets worth of syrup from trees in the Sugarbush area.

The Wildflower Garden is at its most beautiful during spring. Although most of the plantings are found in a woodland area, displays of native plants are also found in different ecosystems such as bogs, prairies, sand barrens, and cliff faces. These areas are planted with over 500 plants indigenous to Ohio.

The Rhododendron Garden was planted in the early 1970s. It covers approximately forty acres and includes small ponds, a beech and oak woodland area (which holds two of the oldest trees in The Arboretum, a 350-year-old white oak and a 250-year-old red oak), as well as many members of the heath family, rhododendrons, and azaleas. Common varieties as well as rare species are found here. One of the most unusual is the Makino Rhododendron, found only in a few gardens outside of its native Japan.

In 1989 The Holden Arboretum developed its "Master Plan 2000," defining goals and visions for the decades to come. As funds have become available, The Arboretum is poised on the brink of an exciting time of growth and development. Three areas are of particular importance: stewardship of the land, the quality of each visitor's experience, and the importance of the scientific mission at Holden.

In 1930 E. H. Wilson, a renowned botanist from the Arnold Arboretum in Boston, viewed the new site for The Holden Arboretum and assured Mrs. Roberta Holden Bole, sister of Albert Fairchild Holden, that "you will someday have the greatest arboretum in the world." It is a statement that today The Holden Arboretum is convinced will come true.

The Morton Arboretum*

Lisle, Illinois

THE CHOICE OF a family motto often offers a glimpse into what values the family considers to be most important. Throughout the ages honor, valor, and integrity have been common themes. Although these principles were also important for the J. Sterling Morton family, their motto—"Plant Trees"—says what was closest to their hearts and souls.

Julius Sterling Morton was born in New York in 1832 and raised in Michigan. When he moved to the Nebraska territory in 1854 he bought a farmstead and built what was eventually known as Arbor Lodge. He lived a long and interesting life, and at various times was a businessman, railroad promoter, newspaper editor, and farmer. His political career culminated in his appointment as Secretary of Agriculture under President Grover Cleveland.

Morton's love of nature inspired him to plant the bleak landscape of his Nebraska property with rich and varied collections of trees and shrubs. He began the institution of Arbor Day, first celebrated in 1872, in Nebraska.

Joy Morton was the eldest of four sons of J. Sterling Morton and his wife Caroline Joy. The boys lived in Nebraska and were raised in the tradition of their parents' love of nature.

In 1876 Morton, accompanied by his son Joy, traveled to Boston for the centennial celebration. While there, they visited the new Arnold Arboretum, which had opened only four years earlier. The Arboretum impressed both father and son, and Joy returned to Nebraska resolved to one day create such a place in the Midwest.

Joy put this dream on hold during his years in business. In 1879 he moved to Aurora, Illinois, to work for the Chicago, Burlington, and Quincy Railroad. While he was there, he met E. I. Wheeler, who owned a salt company; Joy joined the company as junior partner and when Mr. Wheeler died in 1885, Joy bought the remaining interests and formed what was eventually known as the Morton Salt Company.

In spite of his business success, Joy Morton had not forgotten the love of nature he had learned as a child. He began looking for land for a country estate. In 1909, while helping to put out a brush fire in Du Page County, north of Lisle, Illinois, Joy and his business associate E. A. Potter discovered a perfect building site. Soon the Mortons' country estate was begun.

Many of the parcels of land bought by Joy Morton were old farmsteads that had been cut, cleared,

and used for pastureland for years. Other pieces were virtually untouched. He united the land holdings and called it the Lisle Farms Company.

The house that the Mortons built on this land was a half-timber, three-story building they called Thornhill. Other existing farm buildings soon became known as the Home Farm.

It is not clearly known what The Arboretum land looked like before the arrival of European settlers. It is believed that much of the land was forest. Early settlers referred to the forested area on the west side of the Du Page River as Parsons' Grove. That on the east side was known as King's Grove. These areas were composed primarily of sugar maple, with white ash, hop hornbeam, basswood, and red oak. The forest floor was thought to have been covered with woodland treasures such as bloodroot, toothwort, bellwort, Dutchman's breeches,

hepatica, and trout lily. Natural prairie was found on this land only at the far eastern end, in a northeast corner and along a ragged edge to the south.

Researchers at The Arboretum guess that in the early years of the nineteenth century, more than 500 different species of plants could be found on the land that belongs to The Arboretum today.

Joy and his son, Sterling, began to think more seriously about establishing an arboretum on the property near Lisle. In 1920, while Joy was traveling in Europe, Sterling wrote on behalf of his father to Dr. Charles S. Sargent, director of the Arnold Arboretum. He asked Dr. Sargent if he thought an area twenty-five miles from the city would attract enough visitors to make the creation of a public arboretum worthwhile. Dr. Sargent's answer was an enthusiastic *yes!*

Acting on the advice of Dr. Sargent, Joy Morton

hired Ossian Cole Simonds, a well-known landscape architect from Chicago, to help with the initial plan of The Arboretum. Simonds, like his contemporary Jens Jensen, believed in a naturalistic style of architecture. In 1908 Simonds began teaching landscape design courses at the University of Michigan. In his 1920 book, *Landscape Gardening,* he encouraged not only pupils but also the general public to use their natural surroundings as inspiration for garden design and to "respect the wooded bluffs and hillsides, the springs, streams, riverbanks, and lakeshores within the city boundaries and preserve them with tender loving care."

In keeping with this emphasis on maintaining the integrity of the geographic terrain, O. C. Simonds designed The Morton Arboretum in a naturalistic style.

Actual work to change Thornhill from a country estate to a world-class arboretum began in 1921, when men with a team of mules slowly began to widen and deepen a small tributary of the Du Page River to create the first of several lakes that would beautify the land. Mr. Simonds directed the creation of Lake Marmo (named for Joy Morton's wife, Margaret Morton) and Lake Jopamaca (named for the beginning letters of each of J. Sterling son's names: Joy, Paul, Mark, and Carl.)

Much of the actual field work was supervised by Clarence E. Godshalk, a graduate of the University of Michigan in landscape design. Godshalk, who worked directly for Joy Morton, proved to be an invaluable addition to the early Arboretum staff. He was next appointed Arboretum superintendent, and eventually director of The Arboretum.

The deed of trust written by Joy Morton in 1922 stated that the purpose of The Arboretum was "for practical scientific research work in horticulture and agriculture, particularly in the growth and culture of trees, shrubs, vines and grasses, by means of a great outdoor museum . . . in order to increase the general knowledge and love of trees and shrubs, and bring about an increase and improvement in their growth and culture."

Staff and volunteers at The Morton Arboretum today try to hold true to these original ideas put forth by the founder over seven decades ago.

The Morton Arboretum covers 1,500 acres and includes over 3,000 kinds of woody plants from around the world. These plants are divided into four specific groups: botanical, landscape, geographic, and natural areas.

The land purchased for The Arboretum includes many different ecosystems, so it was determined that the botanical collections should be planted in the areas best suited to their growth, rather than planted in groups based on evolutionary order. It was also decided that since The Arboretum was developed not only for the display of botanical families, but also for educating the public about landscaping and horticulture, each group would be shown with other plants that shared similar cultural requirements, thus providing inspiration for creating gardens, rather than mere collections.

A tour of The Morton Arboretum begins with the Horticulture Display Gardens, located south of the Visitor Center. In this garden home gardeners as well as professional nurserymen and landscape designers can study plants and combinations of plants, both familiar and unusual, suitable for growing in Illinois.

RIGHT. *Iris* (Iris sp.).

OPPOSITE. *Joy Morton began work on the Arboretum in 1921, hiring O. C. Simonds, a landscape architect of the Jens Jensen school, to design the land in a naturalistic style.*

In the center of this area, originally planted in 1934, is a formal hedge garden where over fifty-five different woody plants are trimmed into hedges. Four white columns stand at the east end of the garden; these represent the four sons of J. Sterling Morton. At the west end, the patio and rotunda of the Administration Building create a graceful focal point.

An old-fashioned rose garden was first planted in the center of the hedge garden in 1936, but as the elm trees that border the garden became taller, they began to shade out the roses, which were eventually removed.

The Ground-cover Garden is particularly popular with gardeners who want to determine how these attractive, low-growing plants can best be used in the landscape. It is divided into two different areas: on one side of a brick path, the beds are planted with ground covers and companion plants that thrive in shade; on the other side are plants that need full sun.

Perhaps one of the most special places in this horticultural museum is the May T. Watts Reading Garden, named for a former Arboretum naturalist. Located just outside the Sterling Morton Library, it is a beautiful little walled garden that provides visitors a place to sit and read outdoors. Many of the plants used in this garden are important in the history and development of horticulture, giving the impression that one is in the midst of a living book.

The Geographic Trail takes the visitor around the world. Collections along this trail display plants indigenous to various regions of the earth, including central and western Asia, China, Japan, the Balkans, eastern United States wetlands, and the Appalachians.

The collections are not planted according to landscape styles of these various countries and regions, but are grouped in the naturalistic style characteristic of The Morton Arboretum. Because central Illinois may not offer the conditions in which many

ABOVE AND OPPOSITE. *Flowering shrubs, such as this rhododendron, add soft color to the woods in early summer.*

of these plants grow in their native homes, special
beds were amended with sand, peat, rocks, and other
additives to meet the individual cultural needs of
these plants. Many of the collections were laid out in
the early 1920s and have been thriving ever since. The
Appalachian area, planted in the early 1980s, is the
most recent addition.

Plants in the same family or genus grow together
in the Botanical Group collection. Some of the more

interesting or important plant families displayed
are the Rose, Maple, Oak, Willow, Olive, and Dogwood collections.

The Special Habitat Groups are collections of
plants that grow naturally together in a particular
ecosystem. For example, the sand beds display plants,
such as prickly-pear cactus and sandy black oak, that
grow in warm, well-drained soils.

Although the display gardens and plant collections form the backbone of The Arboretum, research and education also play a vital role. Currently research at The Morton Arboretum involves investigation of the effects of urbanization on native oaks, and improved breeding and selection of such popular trees as elms, maples, and rhododendrons.

Educational opportunities at The Morton Arboretum include interpretive programs, lectures, classes, and workshops for all ages. Natural history, many botanical topics, horticulture, and landscaping are all explored in these programs.

The people at The Morton Arboretum like to say that every day is Arbor Day here, and truly the planting and promoting of trees in the landscape is a theme that runs through every program, every event at The Arboretum throughout the year.

J. Sterling Morton, who first began Arbor Day in Nebraska in 1872, once said, "Arbor Day is not like other holidays. Each of those reposes on the past, while Arbor Day proposes for the future."

This is true not only of Arbor Day but also of the legacy which Sterling Morton left his son—for Joy Morton lived the family motto of "Planting Trees," and left us all a wonderful proposition for the future.

The Paine Art Center and Arboretum*

Oshkosh, Wisconsin

TUCKED AWAY IN a corner of the picturesque town of Oshkosh, Wisconsin, The Paine Art Center and Arboretum is a living tribute to a great and generous man and a lovely place to spend a few quiet hours. The Art Center houses both a permanent collection of paintings and sculpture as well as temporary exhibits that change often. The gardens, also beautiful, change their "exhibits" with the seasons.

The Paine Art Center and Arboretum is a gift to the people of Wisconsin from Nathan Paine, whose grandfather and uncle founded the Paine Lumber Company.

The Paine family had a long tradition of pioneering spirit. It was this spirit and a love of the out-of-doors that inspired Nathan's grandfather and uncle to become interested in the timber business. Buying land from the railroad company, the Paine Lumber Company eventually acquired 52,000 acres and ran their own logging camps and railroad.

After their father died in 1917, Nathan and his brother Edward took over the company and worked diligently, enjoying great financial success. Having personally benefited from the success of the company, Nathan soon felt the need to give something back to the community, particularly to the 2,000 men and women who worked for the Paine Lumber Company. Seemingly tireless in his community efforts, he organized cultural events, a monthly company magazine, a band, and an athletic team.

The idea of building a quiet, country home came to him one day when he was looking over timberland in northern Wisconsin. He happened onto a cleared area where a lumber camp had once been. The clearing was surrounded by a beautiful grove of native trees, and Paine was struck by the peace and solitude that such a setting provided.

Inspired by the vision of this place of natural beauty, Nathan and his wife Jessie Kimberly Paine commissioned Bryant Fleming of Ithaca, New York, to design a home and garden that would provide

The Paine Art Center and Arboretum was a gift to the people of Wisconsin from Nathan Paine, whose grandfather and uncle founded the Paine Lumber Company.

OPPOSITE. *The manor, which houses a wonderful art collection, was designed in an English style by Bryant Fleming of Ithaca, New York.*

them with a quiet, beautiful retreat. Fleming was well known in the East for his English-style residences and gardens, and he soon completed plans for formal gardens and a Tudor-style house. The foundation was poured in 1926.

Although Fleming's original plans called for a series of formal gardens with tight, geometrical shapes, this did not fit well with Nathan Paine's memory of a sunny clearing surrounded by wildflowers and native trees. After the house was completed, Fleming and the Paines split ways. Although some of Fleming's ideas were completed— namely the location of the walks, terraces, and balustrades—the remainder of the grounds were designed by Nathan Paine and a local landscape architect, John Roe.

By 1930, the main structure was completed and Nathan Paine was able to see the landscape of his

dreams as he stood on the terrace and looked out onto a sunny clearing, bordered with native trees and shrubs.

Unfortunately the Depression took its toll on the Paines, and they were never able to move into the mansion they had built. Over the next seventeen years, until Nathan Paine's death in 1947, the doors remained closed. During those years, however, Nathan Paine took necessary measures to assure that the house and gardens in Oshkosh would be well preserved. He organized two corporations, The Paine Art Center and Arboretum, and the Algoma Realty Company. Portions of the latter were then liquidated to establish an endowment for the former.

After her husband's death, Jessie Kimberly Paine was determined to open the Art Center and Arboretum to the public. Although she chose not to live there, she authorized the completion of the building and the unpacking of the priceless works of art that they had purchased for the Art Center.

The party celebrating the formal opening of The Paine Art Center and Arboretum was typical of the Paines' generosity and respect for the working man. The first group invited to the Center were the workmen who had helped create the mansion and the grounds.

Mrs. Paine remained actively involved with the Center until her death, at age 100, in 1973. At that time the grounds were redesigned and greatly changed. It was decided to change the landscape from an arboretum consisting primarily of woody plants to a botanical garden displaying more colorful annuals, perennials, and typical garden plants, in the hope of attracting more visitors to the Center and educating the community about plants they could use in their own gardens.

One of the most beautiful of all the additions to the grounds is the sunken formal English garden. This is a nearly exact copy of the Dutch Pond Garden at Hampton Court, England. The central fountain was

The Paines never lived in the mansion, which was completed in 1930. In 1947, Jessie Kimberly Paine opened it to the public as an art center.

A small carriage house (to the right) next to the English Garden is now used as a gathering place for classes and lectures.

Blossoms from annuals and perennials paint a colorful picture against a low stone wall in the formal English Garden.

The Paine Art Center and Arboretum

It was Nathan Paine's wish to create a place where people could come and enjoy the peace and solitude of nature that he had discovered as a child.

The formal English Garden is a nearly exact copy of the Dutch Pond Garden at Hampton Court, England.

Arboretums

Statuary and fountains enhance the natural beauty of the garden.

The newest garden, the Children's Garden, is planted with a different theme each year. In 1994 and 1995 the theme was Mr. MacGregor's garden, and all the plants found in the garden were the ones mentioned by Beatrix Potter in her incomparable tale of Peter Rabbit. The plants and architectural features are all child-sized, and only children are allowed to walk through this innovative garden.

Roses were always important to the Paines, who originally planned three rose gardens for the estate. The current rose garden, created in 1988, contains over one hundred hardy shrub roses planted in gently curving beds, mimicking the curves of the reflecting canal around which they grow.

The White Garden is found just outside the breakfast room east of the Great Hall loggia. This garden is planted with dozens of different kinds of plants with white blooms or variegated leaves. Foundation plantings in this garden include star magnolia, Japanese tree lilac, hydrangea, and Korean boxwood.

Nathan Paine's original dream of a naturally wooded setting has not been forgotten, and many informal areas remain on the property. A primrose and wooded path is particularly beautiful in spring as ephemeral woodland wildflowers bloom side by side with cultivated cousins such as daffodils and primrose. The tree and shrub collection is outstanding and offers gardeners the chance to observe how various species withstand the harsh Wisconsin winters. The prairie/woodland garden is located along Highway 110 and Congress Avenue to the west of the Art Center.

The unique blend of horticulture and art found at The Paine Art Center and Arboretum is a treasure for all who visit. From the formal English sunken garden to the wide open spaces of the prairie restoration, the gardens at The Paine Center could not be more beautiful if they had been painted with an artist's brush.

donated by the Wisconsin National Life Insurance Company, and is surrounded by thousands of flowering bulbs and annuals during spring and summer. An upper tier was made into an expansive perennial border, inspired by Gertrude Jekyll's garden border at Munstead Wood in England.

The annual beds are often used as a test site for the All-American Selections. This, too, is in keeping with the English tradition, for the gardens at Hampton Court and other English manors were used to display new species that plant explorers brought from all over the world.

West of the carriage house is another formal area, the Herb Garden. Two intersecting red brick paths effectively cut the garden into four main areas in which culinary, medicinal, aromatic, and ornamental herbs are grown.

Appendices

Suggested Tours

Travel with a focus makes for expeditions that are both interesting and educational, whether you journey far away or make a day trip from your own home. The gardens in this book offer visitors the opportunity to see visually stunning horticultural displays and the chance to learn about gardening, plants, and nature.

The gardens described in each chapter are grouped according to type rather than by geography. To help make it easy for readers to tour these gardens, this section outlines six trips, each covering as many gardens as possible in the same general area. The gardens with the most spectacular horticultural displays are marked with an asterisk (*). Following these lists, specific travel information about each garden is given alphabetically by state.

1. Kentucky and Indiana

LEXINGTON, KENTUCKY
 *Ashland *(page 139)*
 Lexington Cemetery *(page 97)*

HARRODSBURG, KENTUCKY
(25 miles southwest of Lexington)
 Shaker Village of Pleasant Hill *(page 84)*

CLERMONT, KENTUCKY
(70 miles west of Harrodsburg;
25 miles south of Louisville)
 Bernheim Arboretum and Research Forest *(page 198)*

LOUISVILLE, KENTUCKY
(25 miles north of Clermont)
 Cave Hill Cemetery *(page 95)*

INDIANAPOLIS, INDIANA
(113 miles north of Louisville)
 *Eli Lilly Garden *(page 108)*

NEW HARMONY, INDIANA
(130 miles southwest of Indianapolis)
 New Harmony *(page 90)*

2. Illinois and Missouri

EVANSTON, ILLINOIS
(12 miles north of Chicago)
 *Shakespeare Garden *(page 74)*

WILMETTE, ILLINOIS
(5 miles north of Evanston)
 Baha'i House of Worship *(page 92)*

GLENCOE, ILLINOIS
(12 miles north of Wilmette)
 *Chicago Botanic Garden *(page 27)*

WHEATON, ILLINOIS
(30 miles west of Chicago)
 *Cantigny *(page 172)*

LISLE, ILLINOIS
(25 miles west of Chicago,
5 miles north of Wheaton)
 The Morton Arboretum *(page 212)*

ST. LOUIS, MISSOURI
(300 miles southwest of Chicago)
 *Missouri Botanical Garden *(page 16)*

AREA OF DETAIL

MINNESOTA

DULUTH

WISCONSIN

MICHIGAN

Noerenberg
Gardens

MINNEAPOLIS
ST. PAUL

The Paine Art Center
and Arboretum

Dow Gardens

Minnesota Landscape
Arboretum

Boerner
Botanical Garden

Mitchell Park
Conservatory

Chicago
Botanic Garden

Michigan State
University Gardens

Old World
Wisconsin

MILWAUKEE

Baha'i House
of Worship

LANSING

Cranbrook House
and Gardens

IOWA

The Morton
Arboretum

Shakespeare Garden

DETROIT

The Holden Arboretum

DES MOINES

Cantigny

CHICAGO

Cleveland
Botanical Garden

CLEVELAND

Fellows Riverside
Gardens

AKRON

ILLINOIS

Eli Lilly
Garden

Kingwood
Center

Stan Hywet
Hall and Gardens

MISSOURI

SPRINGFIELD

INDIANAPOLIS

COLUMBUS

OHIO

The Dawes
Arboretum

KANSAS CITY

INDIANA

Inniswood
Metro Gardens

CINCINNATI

ST. LOUIS

Cave Hill
Cemetery

LOUISVILLE

Ashland;
Lexington Cemetery

Missouri
Botanical Garden

New Harmony

LEXINGTON

Shaker Village of
Pleasant Hill

KENTUCKY

Bernheim
Arboretum and
Research Forest

400 KM

0

400 MILES

Suggested Tours

3. Michigan

BLOOMFIELD HILLS
(23 miles northwest of Detroit)
  *Cranbrook House and Gardens *(page 166)*

MIDLAND
(105 miles northwest of Bloomfield Hills)
  Dow Gardens *(page 150)*

EAST LANSING
(90 miles south of Midland)
  Michigan State University Gardens:
    W. J. Beal Botanical Garden *(page 60)*
    *Horticultural Demonstration Gardens *(page 56)*
    *4-H Children's Garden *(page 65)*

4. Minnesota

CHANHASSEN
(10 miles west of Minneapolis)
  *Minnesota Landscape Arboretum *(page 187)*

PLYMOUTH
(10 miles north of Chanhassen)
  Noerenberg Gardens *(page 103)*

5. Ohio

CLEVELAND
  *Cleveland Botanical Garden *(page 46)*

MENTOR
(25 miles east of Cleveland)
  The Holden Arboretum *(page 207)*

MANSFIELD
(80 miles southwest of Cleveland)
  *Kingwood Center *(page 143)*

COLUMBUS
(67 miles south of Mansfield)
  Inniswood Metro Gardens *(page 129)*

NEWARK
(40 miles east of Columbus)
  The Dawes Arboretum *(page 192)*

AKRON
(90 miles northeast of Newark)
  Stan Hywet Hall and Gardens *(page 156)*

YOUNGSTOWN
(48 miles east of Akron)
  Fellows Riverside Gardens *(page 114)*

6. Wisconsin

MILWAUKEE
  Mitchell Park Conservatory *(page 123)*

HALES CORNER
(10 miles southwest of Milwaukee)
  *Boerner Botanical Gardens *(page 39)*

OSHKOSH
(86 miles north of Milwaukee)
  The Paine Art Center and Arboretum *(page 219)*

EAGLE
(36 miles west of Milwaukee)
  Old World Wisconsin *(page 79)*

Travel Guide

Illinois

❧ Baha'i House of Worship

Travel Information: The Baha'i House of Worship is
located just off Sheridan Road in Wilmette, Illinois.
From Chicago, drive north to Wilmette.

For information, write Baha'i House of Worship,
Wilmette, IL 60091, or call (708) 853-2300.

Hours: May 1–September 30, 10:00 A.M.–10:00 P.M. daily.
October 1–April 30, 10:00 A.M.–5:00 P.M. daily.

Admission: No fee.

Seasonal Displays: Spring: tulips, lilacs, daffodils.
Summer: daylilies, hydrangea, balloon flower, hibiscus,
tree peonies, petunias. Fall: Mahonia, Joe-Pye weed,
pieris. Winter: evergreens.

❧ Cantigny

Travel Information: Cantigny is located in Wheaton,
Illinois. From the Chicago Loop, go 30 miles west on
Eisenhower and East-West Tollway to Winfield Road.
Follow signs to Cantigny Estate Main Entrance.

For information, write 1 S 151 Winfield Rd., Wheaton,
IL 60187, or call (708) 668-5161.

Gift Shop at Visitor's Center.

Hours: Closed January; February: Open Friday through
Sunday 9:00 A.M.–dusk; March 1–December 29: Open
Tuesday through Sunday 9:00 A.M.–dusk; Closed
Mondays except for select holidays: Open Memorial
Day, Independence Day, Labor Day; Closed Thanks-
giving Day and December 23, 24, 25, 26, 30, 31.

Admission: No fees.

Seasonal Displays: Spring: annuals, early perennials, spring
bulbs, flowering trees and shrubs such as magnolia,
redbud, buckeye, lilacs. Summer: annuals and
perennials, vegetables, herbs. Fall: autumn foliage.
Winter: tree collections, evergreens, berries.

❧ Chicago Botanic Garden

Travel Information: Chicago Botanic Garden is located
25 miles north of downtown Chicago on Lake-Cook
Road in Glencoe, Illinois. Follow the Edens Expressway

(94-41) north to Lake-Cook Road and go east one-half
mile to the entrance.

For information, write P.O. Box 400, Glencoe, IL
60022, or call (708) 835-5440.

Gift shop and restaurant on property.

Hours: Open daily from 8:00 A.M.–sunset.

Admission: No fee; parking $4.00 per car.

Seasonal Displays: Spring: spring bulbs. Summer: aquatic
plants, vegetables, perennials, roses, herbs, annuals.
Fall: foliage in Turnbull Woods, Japanese garden.
Winter: dwarf conifers.

❧ The Morton Arboretum

Travel Information: The Morton Arboretum is located
just north of Lisle, Illinois, at the intersection of Illinois
Route 53 (a main north-south highway) and Illinois
Route 88 (the East-West tollway). Follow the signs
"To Aurora" until you reach the Arboretum exit, which
is well marked.

For information, write The Morton Arboretum,
Lisle, IL, 60532, or call (708) 968-0074.

Gift Shop at Visitor's Center.

Hours: Grounds are open from 7:00 A.M. to 7:00 P.M.
(or dusk, whichever is earlier.)

Admission: Road use and parking fees, $6.00 per car
(Wednesdays are half price).

Seasonal Displays: Spring: daffodils, Virginia bluebells,
fothergilla, redbuds, crabapple, azaleas, magnolias,
wildflowers, lilacs, rhododendrons. Summer: annuals
and perennials in display garden, roses, prairie flowers.
Fall: autumn foliage, prairie flowers. Winter: hedge
garden, evergreens.

❧ Shakespeare Garden

Travel Information: The Shakespeare Garden is located
on the campus of Northwestern University in Evanston,
Illinois. Take Sheridan Road to Garrett Place (between
Noyes St. and Foster St.). Turn east on Garrett Place
and park in the cul-de-sac. Look for the bluestone
walk just to the east of the small Howe Chapel on
Garrett Place. Follow this walk and look for the large

sign saying "Shakespeare Garden" which directs one through an arbor of shrubbery to the garden.

For information, write Northwestern University, Office of University Relations, 555 Clark Street, Evanston, IL, 60208, or call (708) 491-4886.

Hours: Open daily.

Admission: No individual fee, $35.00 for guided group tour.

Seasonal Displays: Garden is at its height in spring and early summer. Spring: pansies, daffodils, primula, stock, peonies, columbine, harebell, anemone, ranunculus, dame's rocket. Summer: roses, daisies, iris, pinks, lady's mantle, allium, feverfew, rose campion, daylilies, forget-me-not, hollyhock, monarda, lilies, goatsbeard, mallow, globe thistle, yarrow. Fall: artemisia, alyssum, aster, boltonia, Japanese anemone, monkshood, annual salvia, roses.

Indiana

Eli Lilly Garden

Travel Information: Eli Lilly Garden is found on the grounds of the Indianapolis Museum of Art.

For information, write Indianapolis Museum of Art, 1200 West 38th Street, Indianapolis, IN 46208-4196, or call (317) 923-1331.

Gift shop at the main museum building.

Hours: The grounds are open to the public from 5:00 A.M. to 8:00 P.M. daily.

Admission: No fee.

Seasonal Displays: Spring: daffodils and other spring bulbs. Summer: perennials and annuals. Fall: autumn foliage.

New Harmony

Travel Information: New Harmony is located on the Wabash River at the intersection of Indiana Routes 66 and 68. From Interstate 64 in Indiana, take the Poseyville exit; in Illinois, take the Grayville exit, south on Highway 1 to Highway 14.

For information, write Earthcare, North Street, New Harmony, IN 47631, or call (812) 682-5136.

Restaurant, inn, gift shop, and library reading room available at the gardens.

Hours: Gardens open dawn to dusk daily. Earthcare at the Depot (garden center) hours: Tuesday through Saturday 10:00 A.M.–4:00 P.M.; Sunday 1:00 P.M.–4:00 P.M. Inquire about winter hours beginning November 1.

Admission: No fees.

Seasonal Displays: Spring: Iris, hollyhocks, peonies, and foxglove. Summer: daylilies, prairie demonstration area, hostas, rose garden, golden rain tree. Fall: Prairie flowers.

Kentucky

Ashland

Travel Information: The gardens at Ashland are located on the grounds of the estate of Henry Clay, 120 Sycamore Road (corner of Richmond Road).

For information, write Ashland, 120 Sycamore Road, Lexington, KY 40502, or call (606) 266-8581.

Gift shop located in the main house.

Hours: The garden is open from dawn until dusk, daily.

Admission: No fee.

Seasonal Displays: Spring: peonies, tulips, coral bells, small fruit trees. Summer: roses, pink lycorias, white phlox, begonias, herbs. Fall: anemone, autumn crocus, fall asters, chrysanthemums. Winter: Trees of interest: yellow wood tree, white ash, large firechief holly, hornbeams, boxwood.

Bernheim Arboretum and Research Forest

Travel Information: Bernheim is located 25 miles south of Louisville, Kentucky, on I-65. Take the Bardstown-Clermont exit (No. 112) and go east on KY 245 for one mile. Bernheim is 15 miles west of Bardstown on KY 245.

For information, write Bernheim Arboretum and Research Forest, Highway 245, Clermont, KY 40110, or call (502) 955-8512.

Hours: March 15–November 14, Monday–Saturday 9:00 A.M.–5:00 P.M., Sunday 12:00 P.M.–4:00 P.M. During Eastern Daylight Time, Bernheim is open Monday–Saturday 10:00 A.M.–7:00 P.M., Sunday 12:00 P.M.–7:00 P.M. November 15–March 14, Saturday and Sunday 12:00 P.M.–4:00 P.M.

Admission: No fee, Monday through Friday. $5.00 per vehicle Saturday, Sunday, and holidays.

Seasonal Displays: Spring: flowering crabapples, dogwoods, magnolias, viburnum, azaleas, rhododendrons, wild flowers, lilac, beech, perennials. Summer: annuals and perennials, hydrangeas, golden rain tree, butterfly bush, herbs, ornamental grasses, water lilies. Fall: leaf and berry colors. Winter: Holly, dwarf conifers, witch hazel, ornamental grasses.

Cave Hill Cemetery

Travel Information: Cave Hill Cemetery is located at the east end of Broadway in downtown Louisville.

For information, write Cave Hill Cemetery, 701 Baxter Avenue, Louisville, KY 40204, or call (502) 451-5330.
Hours: Open daily, 8:00 A.M.–4:45 P.M. (weather permitting).

Lexington Cemetery

Travel Information: Lexington Cemetery is located in downtown Lexington.

For information, write Lexington Cemetery, 833 West Main Street, Lexington, KY 40508, or call (606) 255-5522.
Hours: Office open Monday through Saturday, 8:00 A.M.–4:00 P.M., Sunday 1:00 P.M.–4:00 P.M.

Shaker Village of Pleasant Hill*

Travel Information: Shaker Village is located on U.S. Highway 68, 25 miles southwest of Lexington and 7 miles northeast of Harrodsburg, Kentucky.

For information, write Shaker Village of Pleasant Hill, 3501 Lexington Road, Harrodsburg, KY 40330, or call (606) 734-5411.
Craft and gift shop at Visitors Center, dining at the Trustees' Inn, lodging available in 15 restored Shaker buildings (reservations required).
Hours: The village is open year round except for Christmas Eve and Christmas Day. April through October: 9:30 A.M.–5:00 P.M. Winter hours vary—call ahead.
Seasonal Displays: Spring: damask and apothecary roses. Summer: herbs (yellow, red and white yarrow, foxglove, lavender, butterfly weed, lythrum, baptisia, calendula, feverfew, echinacea) and vegetables. Fall: Harvested herbs on display at Farm Deacon Shop.

Michigan

Cranbrook House and Gardens

Travel Information: Cranbrook House and Gardens are located at 380 Lone Pine Road, east of Telegraph (U.S. 24) and west of Woodward Avenue (M-1). Park on Lone Pine Road immediately across from the entrance gates, or in the Christ Church Cranbrook parking lot.

For information, write Cranbrook Educational Community, 380 Lone Pine Road, P.O. Box 801, Bloomfield Hills, MI 48303-0801, or call (810) 645-3149.

Hours: May–August 10:00 A.M.–5:00 P.M. Monday–Saturday, 11:00 A.M.–5:00 P.M. Sunday; September: 1:00 P.M.–5:00 P.M. Monday–Saturday, 11:00 A.M.–5:00 P.M. Sunday. October: weekends only 12:00 P.M.–4:00 P.M. Closed November–April.
Admission: No fee.
Seasonal Displays: Spring: tulips in sunken garden, wildflowers, azaleas, rhododendrons. Summer: annuals, perennials, herbs, hostas, reflecting pool garden, Oriental garden. Fall: chrysanthemums, autumn foliage.

Dow Gardens

Travel Information: Dow Gardens are located in Midland, Michigan. From Business Route 10 take Eastman Avenue south to St. Andrews Road. The Midland Center for the Arts and entrance to Dow Gardens is at this intersection.

For information, write 1018 West Main Street, Midland, MI 48640, or call (517) 631-2677.
Gift shop located in Art Center building.
Hours: The Gardens are open 10:00 A.M. until sunset, daily. Closed Thanksgiving, Christmas, and New Years Day.
Admission: Daily admission pass is $2.00.
Seasonal Displays: Spring: crocus, tulips, daffodils, magnolias, crabapples, viburnum, and lilac. Summer: rhododendron, azaleas, roses, annuals and perennials, herbs, wild flowers. Fall: perennials, autumn foliage. Winter: witchhazel.

Michigan State University Horticultural Demonstration Gardens

Travel Information: The Gardens are located on the campus of Michigan State University in East Lansing by the Plant and Soil Sciences Building on the corner of Wilson and Bogue Streets. The main entrance is off Bogue Street, south of Wilson Road, and north of Service Drive. Parking is available in the Garden's visitor lot off Bogue Street. During University business hours (8:00 A.M.–5:00 P.M. weekdays) tokens must be purchased for $1.00.

For information, and to arrange a group tour, write Garden Manager, Department of Horticulture, Plant and Soil Sciences Building, East Lansing, MI 48824, or call (517) 355-0348.
Gift store at Visitors Information Center behind Plant and Soil Sciences Building.
Hours: Gardens are open all year from sunup to sundown,

although access may be limited November–April. Teaching greenhouses are open Monday through Friday from 8:00 A.M. to 4:30 P.M.

Admission: No individual fees. Small fee charged for guided tours, call to schedule at least two weeks in advance.

Seasonal Displays: Spring: roses, bulbs, spring annuals (pansies), early perennials, iris. Summer: full color and height of bloom of annuals and perennials mid to late summer. Fall: chrysanthemums, ornamental grasses, hybrid Japanese anemones, sedum, and other fall blooming perennials.

✀ Michigan State University 4-h Children's Garden

Travel Information: The 4-h Children's Garden is located on the campus of Michigan State University adjacent to the Plant and Soil Sciences Building on the southwest corner of Wilson Road and Bogue Street in East Lansing.

For information, write Michigan 4-h Children's Garden, 4-h Foundation, 4700 South Hagadorn Road, Suite 220, East Lansing, MI 48823, or call (517) 353-6692. To schedule a tour, call (517) 355-0348.

Hours: Open 7:00 A.M. to 10:00 P.M. daily, May 1–October 31.

Admission: No fee. $1.00 parking tokens (available in Visitor Center behind Plant and Soil Sciences Building) necessary weekdays until 5:30 P.M.

Seasonal Displays: Spring: spring bulbs, early perennials and annuals, early vegetables in kitchen garden. Summer: vegetables, summer annuals, butterfly garden, evening primrose. Fall: late perennials, fall vegetables.

✀ Michigan State University W. J. Beal Botanical Garden

Travel Information: W. J. Beal Botanical Garden is located on the campus of Michigan State University in East Lansing. Take Route 127 north to Kalamazoo Street, turn right (east) onto campus. Park in public parking lot next to the football stadium and walk across the foot bridge over the Red Cedar River. Go down stairs toward the Garden.

For information, write W. J. Beal Botanical Garden, Michigan State University, East Lansing, MI 48824, or call (517) 355-9582.

Hours: Open dawn until dusk daily throughout the year

Admission: No fee.

Seasonal Displays: Spring: wildflowers, azaleas, rhododendrons. Summer: economic plants, dye plants, endangered plant collection Fall: autumn foliage.

Minnesota

✀ Minnesota Landscape Arboretum

Travel Information: The Arboretum is located west of Chanhassen, 9 miles west of I-494 on State Highway 5. The entrance is on the left, ½ mile west of intersection of Highway 41 and Highway 5.

For information, write Minnesota Landscape Arboretum, 3675 Arboretum Drive, P.O. Box 39, Chanhassen, MN 55317, or call (612) 443-2460.

Gift shop and restaurant in Visitor's Center.

Hours: Grounds are open November 1–March 31, 8:00 A.M.–5:30 P.M., April 1–October 31, 8:00 A.M.–9:00 P.M. Building and library are open all year, 8:00 A.M.–4:30 P.M. weekdays, 11:00 A.M.–4:30 P.M. weekends. The Arboretum is closed Thanksgiving, Christmas Day, New Years Day, and Martin Luther King Day. Call for other holiday hours.

Admission: Small fee for adults and children over 12; free to children under 12.

Seasonal Displays: Spring: daffodils, flowering trees, iris, tulips, wildflowers, azaleas. Summer: annual beds, daylilies, roses, perennials, herbs, peonies, potentilla, viburnum, vegetables. Fall: fruit and autumn foliage. Winter: evergreens.

✀ Noerenberg Gardens

Travel Information: Noerenberg Gardens are located on the northern shore of Lake Minnetonka near Minneapolis, Minnesota. From I-494 take Highway 12 west, County Road 15 south, then County Road 51 west.

For information, write Hennepin Parks, 12615 County Road 9, Plymouth, MN 55441-1248, or call (612) 559-9000. For group tours or wedding reservations, call (612) 559-6700.

Hours: Summer: 7:00 A.M.–8:00 P.M. weekdays, 8:00 A.M.–8:00 P.M. weekends, Autumn: 8:00 A.M.–sunset weekdays, 9:00 A.M.–6:00 P.M. weekends. The park closes for winter from mid-October through the end of April.

Admission: No fee.

Seasonal Displays: Spring: wildflowers, peony, mertensia,

scilla, hellebores, redbud, azalea, magnolia. Summer: cleome, verbena, and many unusual annuals and perennials. Fall: asters, hydrangeas, hosta, ornamental grasses, autumn foliage.

Missouri

❧ MISSOURI BOTANICAL GARDEN

Travel Information: Missouri Botanical Garden is located in St. Louis, Missouri. From I-44 East or I 64 / US 40 East or West, exit at Kings Highway south to Vandeventer. Turn left on Vandeventer, and go right 1½ blocks on Shaw Boulevard.

For information, write P.O. Box 299, St. Louis, MO 63166-0299, or call (314) 577-9400 for pre-recorded information or (314) 577-5141.

Gift shop and restaurant on premises.

Hours: Gardens and conservatories open Memorial Day–Labor Day 9:00 A.M.–8:00 P.M., all other days 9:00 A.M.–5:00 P.M. Early morning hours: Wednesdays and Saturdays, 7:00 A.M.–9:00 A.M. Closed Christmas Day.

Admission: Gardens and conservatories: $3.00; senior citizens, $1.50; children under 12, free. Free admission Wednesday and Saturday before noon, and Monday through Thursday after 5:00 P.M.

Seasonal Displays: Spring: tulips, daffodils, weeping cherries, azaleas, rhododendrons, flowering trees, iris, peonies. Summer: roses, lilies, daylilies, summer annuals, lotus, canna, calla lilies, hosta, perennial beds, scented garden, dahlias, water lilies. Fall: fall fruits, wildflowers, vegetable harvest, chrysanthemums, autumn foliage, Japanese garden. Winter: Climatron, desert house, holly berries, holiday flower show, witch hazel, camellias, indoor orchid show.

Ohio

❧ CLEVELAND BOTANICAL GARDEN

Travel Information: Cleveland Botanical Garden (formerly the Garden Center of Greater Cleveland) is located at 11030 East Boulevard in University Circle, close to the Cleveland Museum of Art, fifteen minutes east of downtown Cleveland.

For information, write Cleveland Botanical Garden, 11030 East Boulevard, Cleveland, OH 44106, or call (216) 721-1600.

Gift shop in Visitor's Center.

Hours: Gardens are open every day from dawn until dusk. Building is open Monday–Friday 9:00 A.M. to 5:00 P.M., Saturday 12:00 P.M.–5:00 P.M., Sunday 1:00 P.M.–5:00 P.M.

Admission: No fee.

Seasonal Displays: Spring: wildflowers. Summer: herbs, perennials, roses. Fall: Japanese garden, autumn foliage along woods trail, herbs.

❧ THE DAWES ARBORETUM

Travel Information: The Dawes Arboretum is located on Ohio Route 13, 3 miles north of I-70, exit 132. The Arboretum is approximately 40 miles east of Columbus.

For information, write 7770 Jacksontown Road, Newark, OH 43056-9380, or call (614) 323-2355 or 1-800-44-DAWES.

Hours: The Arboretum grounds are open dawn until dusk everyday except Thanksgiving, Christmas, and New Years Day. The Visitors Center is open weekdays 8:00 A.M.–5:00 P.M. Saturdays 9:00 A.M.–5:00 P.M. Sundays and holidays 1:00 P.M.–5:00 P.M.

Admission: No fee.

Seasonal Displays: Spring: flowering crabapples, azaleas and rhododendrons, dogwoods. Summer: annuals and perennials, Japanese garden, cypress swamp. Fall: foliage throughout the grounds. Winter: holly, conifer and rare tree collections, Maple Syrup Trail.

❧ FELLOWS RIVERSIDE GARDENS

Travel Information: Fellows Riverside Gardens are located near Youngstown, Ohio. Take the Belle Vista exit off I-680 and follow the signs to Mill Creek Park by going south on Belle Vista and east on Mahoning Avenue.

For information, write Fellows Riverside Gardens, Mill Creek Metropolitan Park District, 816 Glenwood Avenue, Youngstown, OH 44502, or call (216) 743-7275.

Gift shop at Visitor's Center.

Hours: Monday–Friday 10:00 A.M.–4:30 P.M. year round, Saturdays 12:00 P.M.–4:00 P.M., April–mid December, Sundays 1:00 P.M.–5:00 P.M. April–mid December.

Admission: No fee.

Seasonal Displays: Spring: narcissus, crocus, tulips, flowering crabapples. Summer: roses, unusual annuals and perennials, rhododendron collection. Fall: autumn foliage. Winter: dwarf conifers, beech collection.

❧ The Holden Arboretum

Travel Information: The Holden Arboretum is located 25 miles east of Cleveland. Exit at Route 306 off Route I-90. Travel south to Kirtland-Chardon Road, turn east and follow signs to Sperry Road.

For information, write The Holden Arboretum, 9500 Sperry Road, Mentor, OH 44060-8199, or call (216) 946-4400.

Hours: The arboretum is open year round, Tuesday–Sunday 10:00 A.M.–5:00 P.M.

Admission: Adults, $2.50; Senior citizens, $1.75; Children 6–15, $1.75; children under 6, free.

Seasonal Displays: Spring: magnolias, wildflowers, crab apples, lilacs, rhododendrons, azaleas. Summer: perennials, prairie garden. Fall: fall foliage from maple, tupelo, sassafras and oak, fruits. Winter: evergreens.

❧ Inniswood Metro Gardens

Travel Information: Inniswood Metro Gardens are located near Westerville, Ohio. From I-270 take the Route 3 exit, and travel south to the first light, Dempsey Road. Turn left and go to the second light and turn left again on South Hempstead Rd.

For information, write 940 South Hempstead Road, Westerville, OH 43081, or call the Metropolitan Park district at (614) 891-0700.

Hours: Open every day 7:00 A.M. until dark.

Admission: No fee.

Seasonal Displays: Spring: daffodils, rock garden, wildflowers, flowering trees and shrubs, spring perennials. Summer: roses, daylilies, perennials, herbs, hosta. Fall: roses, chrysanthemums, autumn color, witch hazel. Winter: nature trails.

❧ Kingwood Center

Travel Information: Kingwood Center is located in Mansfield, Ohio, on Route 430 (Park Avenue West) with easy access from Route 30 and Route 71.

For information, write Kingwood Center, 900 Park Avenue West, Mansfield, OH 44906, or call (419) 522-0211. Gift shop in Kingwood Hall.

Hours: Easter–October 31: gardens open daily 8:00 A.M. until half-hour before sunset. Greenhouse open daily 8:00 A.M. until one hour before sunset. Kingwood Hall, Tuesday through Saturday 9:00 A.M.–5:00 P.M., Sunday 1:30 P.M.–4:30 P.M. November 1–Easter: gardens open

8:00 A.M.–5:00 P.M. daily. Greenhouse 8:00 A.M.–4:30 P.M. daily. Kingwood Hall, Tuesday through Saturday, 9:00 A.M.–5:00 P.M., closed on Sundays.

Admission: No fee.

Seasonal Displays: Spring: tulips, daffodils, crocus naturalized in woodlands, flowering trees and shrubs, azaleas, rhododendrons. Summer: perennials, roses, iris, peonies, daylilies, annuals, shade garden. Fall: perennials, autumn foliage, roses, greenhouse seasonal display. Winter: greenhouse seasonal display, evergreens.

❧ Stan Hywet Hall and Gardens

Travel Information: Stan Hywet Hall and Gardens are located in Akron, 20 minutes south of the Ohio Turnpike. Take exits 11 or 12 from the Turnpike, or take I-77 North to Route 18. Follow signs to North Portage Path.

For information, write Stan Hywet Hall and Gardens, 714 N. Portage Path, Akron, OH 44303, or call (216) 836-5533.

Hours: Tours Tuesday–Saturday 10:00 A.M.–4:00 P.M., Sunday 1:00 P.M.–4:00 P.M. Grounds open at 9:00 A.M. during summer. Closed Mondays and all major holidays.

Admission: Adults, $7.00; Senior Citizens, $6.50; Children 6–12, $3.50; Children under 6, free.

Seasonal Displays: Spring: daffodils, hyacinths, forsythia, tulips, wild flowers, rhododendron, azaleas. Summer: annuals, perennials, roses, day lilies, peonies (early summer). Fall: annuals, perennials, roses, chrysanthemums. Winter: Conservatory displays, greenhouses can be enjoyed throughout the year.

Wisconsin

❧ Boerner Botanical Gardens

Travel Information: Boerner Botanical Gardens are located in Hales Corners, approximately 10 miles southwest of downtown Milwaukee. From I-894 take either Forest Home Avenue south or 84th Street exit south and follow signs to the gardens.

For more information write 5879 South 92nd Street, Hales Corners, WI 53130, or call (414) 425-1130.

Gift shop at the Garden House, open year round except Thanksgiving, Christmas, and New Year's Day.

Hours: The grounds are open 8:00 A.M. to near sunset daily, formal gardens closed November–March.

Admission: No fee; subject to change.

Seasonal Displays: Spring: spring bulbs, wildflowers, bog garden, flowering trees and shrubs, lilacs, peonies, roses, and iris. Summer: daylilies, delphiniums, lilies, phlox, perennials, annuals, herbs, tuberous begonias. Fall: autumn color, roses, chrysanthemums.

Mitchell Park Conservatory

Travel Information: Mitchell Park Conservatory is located in Milwaukee at 524 South Layton Boulevard. From I-794 take exit #309 B and go south on Layton Boulevard.

For information, write Mitchell Parks, 524 South Layton Boulevard, Milwaukee, WI 53215, or call (414) 649-9800.

Gift Shop in Show Dome.

Hours: Open daily 9:00 A.M.–5:00 P.M.

Admission: No fee 9:00 A.M.–10:30 A.M. daily Monday through Friday (except major holidays) for Milwaukee Country residents. All others, $2.50 per adult, $1.25 per child (6–17 years old), seniors, and handicapped. Children under 6, free. All fees subject to change without notice.

Seasonal Displays: Most changes in displays occur in the Show Dome. Spring: azaleas, rhododendrons, spring bulbs, hydrangeas, geraniums. Summer: Summer show, annuals. Fall: chrysanthemums, autumn show. Christmas: Christmas show, poinsettias. Winter: Azaleas, cyclamen.

The Paine Art Center and Arboretum

Travel Information: The Paine Art Center and Arboretum is located at 1410 Algoma Boulevard (intersection of highways 21 and 110) in Oshkosh.

For information, write The Paine Art Center and Arboretum, 1410 Algoma Boulevard, Oshkosh, WI 54901, or call (414) 235-4530.

Gift shop in Paine House.

Hours: Tuesday–Friday, 10:00 A.M.–4:30 P.M.; Saturday and Sunday, 1:00 P.M.–4:30 P.M.; closed Mondays and holidays.

Admission: $3.00 per adult, $2.50 per senior citizen, $2.00 per student, children under 12 years of age are free.

Seasonal Displays: Spring: spring bulbs (tulips), wildflowers, flowering trees and shrubs. Summer: trees (yellowwood, Japanese tree lilac, fringe tree, smokebush, devil's walking stick), annuals, perennials. Fall: autumn foliage.

Old World Wisconsin*

Travel Information: Old World Wisconsin is located 35 miles west of Milwaukee, 55 miles east of Madison, and 75 miles north of Chicago. It is 20 minutes south of I-94 and 20 minutes north of I-43 on Highway 67.

For information, write Old World Wisconsin, S 103 W37890 Highway 67, Eagle, WI 53119, or call (414) 594-2116.

Gift shop and restaurant on premises.

Hours: Open daily May 1–October 31: weekdays 10:00 A.M.–4:00 P.M.; weekends 10:00 A.M.–5:00 P.M. Expanded hours July and August, weekdays 10:00 A.M.–5:00 P.M. December, first three weekends, 1:00 A.M.–4:00 P.M.

Admission: Fees vary; call ahead.

Seasonal Displays: Spring: special events include Plowing and Planting Day. Summer: Scandinavian Midsummer Celebration and Pioneer Threshing. Fall: Autumn on the Farm.

Gardening Notes

Part of the magic of visiting gardens is in trying to duplicate a bit of it in your own gardens at home. The following notes have been written to help you do just that. Each garden is represented by an outstanding plant, group of plants, or design concept. Horticultural information is given to help you incorporate these into your own gardens. Happy Gardening!

Illinois

✂ Baha'i House of Worship

Blazing star, or gayfeathers, has recently claimed huge popularity as a cut flower for the showiness of its tall purple spikes. Although it was introduced to the cut-flower trade from the Netherlands, liatris is native to North America. In addition to its beauty in arrangements and bouquets, this plant is also very showy in perennial beds, as seen in the gardens surrounding the Baha'i House of Worship.

The foliage of liatris is almost as interesting as its flowering spikes. Long, slender, swordlike leaves form a dense mound out of which the flowers grow. The flowers, found along a long stalk, are usually purplish-red. Unlike most blooms on flowering stalks, however, the blossoms open from top to bottom, rather than the other way around. A member of the composite (daisy) family, liatris does not resemble very closely other members of this plant family.

Gayfeathers *(Liatris spicata)*
Although several liatris species are available through the native plant trade, *L. spicata* and its cultivars are the best for the home garden. 'August Glory' has purple-blue flowers and 'Floristan White' has creamy flowers.

How to Grow
Liatris likes full sun and well-drained soils. Root tubers should be planted in fall, 4–6 inches deep. This is hardy from zones 3–9, though it will not tolerate hot, humid conditions in the Southeast. It will preform best if supplied with even moisture, but will also tolerate drought conditions. Treat to an annual application of fertilizer (rotted manure, compost, or all-purpose fertilizer) in mid-spring.

✂ Cantigny

The floral displays at Cantigny provide wave after wave of blossoms in a sea of color from annuals, perennials, bulbs, and flowering shrubs. Among these, poppies stand out boldly, offering big, bright blossoms on tall, slender stems.

Poppies, a stumbling block for Dorothy on her way to see the Wizard of Oz, nevertheless provide great beauty for the late spring and summer garden. Many perennial poppies last for several years in northern and midwestern gardens, but are treated as annuals in southern gardens because they cannot withstand the heat and humidity of the summers.

Iceland Poppy *(Papaver nudicaule)*
This species from the north is widely used in American gardens because of the beauty of its large, silky blossoms. It grows 12–18 inches tall, and its flowers can be nearly 6 inches across. Several cultivars are available, including 'Scarlet Bubbles', which produces 3-inch blossoms in bright red; 'Summer Promise', which contains solid and bicolor flowers; and 'Wonderland Mix', which has brightly colored flowers on slightly shorter stems.

How to Grow
Both the annual and perennial poppies grow well from seed either started indoors or planted directly outside. Oriental poppy seeds need complete darkness to germinate, so cover with black plastic until germination occurs. To prolong the blooming season of annual poppies, sow seeds several times, two weeks apart.

When seedlings are 3–4 inches tall, thin 5–18 inches apart, depending on the mature height of the plant. Poppies prefer dry soil. Do not overwater.

✂ Chicago Botanic Garden

The bearded iris is considered by some to be the most beautiful of all spring flowers. At the Chicago Botanic Garden these exquisite blossoms can be viewed in several different areas.

liatris

Bearded Iris (*Iris* spp.)

The bearded iris occurs in every color except clear red, and flower forms include both frilly and smooth. The name "bearded" was given to this plant because of the fleshy hairs on the outer petals.

Bearded iris are grouped according to height. Standard forms are 28 inches or taller. These are followed by (in descending order of height) median, border, miniature-tall, intermediate and standard dwarf, which grows only to 3–10 inches tall.

Some of the most beautiful irises include 'Titans Glory', with huge bright purple blossoms, growing 37 inches tall; 'Beverly Sills', with pink, frilly petals on 35-inch stems; and 'Victoria Falls', which grows 40 inches tall and has clear blue flowers and a white beard.

How to Grow

Iris rhizomes should be planted in fertile, well-drained soil in full sun. The bed should be well prepared before planting. Well-rotted manure or a 5-10-10 fertilizer should be worked into the soil along with humus and peat moss. After the beds have been worked, they should be allowed to settle for about three weeks before planting.

Rhizomes should be planted in early fall. Plant no more than 1 inch deep, since the roots are easily smothered. To maintain good bloom, divide clumps every 3–4 years.

iris

✼ Shakespeare Garden

Among the flowers that Shakespeare wrote about are the phloxes—lovely to look at, wonderfully fragrant. Sweet-scented phloxes have been cultivated for many centuries and have been used in gardens for ornamentation, as well as in bouquets to delight the senses. In Victorian England, to send a bouquet of phlox to someone meant a declaration of love and a wish for sweet dreams.

The word phlox comes from the Greek word for flame; this plant got its name because of the bright pink and red coloring of its blossoms.

Garden Phlox (*Phlox paniculata*)

Often called the backbone of the summer season, perennial garden phloxes generally bloom from 4–6 weeks in June and July. They grow 2½–3 feet tall, form neat, compact plants, and produce a wonderfully sweet fragrance.

Different phlox cultivars, in colors ranging from white to pink, purple, red, and blue, can extend the blooming season from June through late August.

How to Grow

In years of excessive rainfall, mildew often becomes a problem for phlox. You can avoid the problem by making sure that air circulates freely around the plants and by soaking the roots rather than using a sprinkler when extra moisture is needed.

Seeds from hybrids of *Phlox paniculata* self-sow readily. This presents a problem in that seedlings often go through a process called reversion, meaning that the seedlings rarely stay true to the color of the parent plant. New plants are most often a muddy purple color. To prevent this, pick faded flower heads before the phlox have had a chance to set seed.

All of the phloxes make excellent cut flowers. For best results, give the cut blossoms a long drink in deep water before arranging.

Kentucky and Indiana

✼ Ashland

Within the old brick walls of the formal garden at Ashland, Henry Clay's estate, many of the flowers, such as astilbe, spill out of the planting beds and into the walkways in their exuberance. The flowering spikes of astilbe appear in late spring and add a wave of delicate blossoms to the garden.

Also known as false spirea, astilbe is an excellent plant for the shady garden, blending well with native ferns and wildflowers.

Astilbe (*Astilbe* × *arendsii*)

Most of the astilbes grown in home gardens are cultivars of this hybrid. One breeder, George Arends of West Germany, became somewhat obsessed with astilbes, and between the years 1902 and 1952, introduced 74 different cultivars.

Astilbes today come in a wide range of colors, including pink, red, salmon, lilac, and white. Plant height varies from less than 12 inches to 4½ feet tall. Individual flowers are quite small but occur in masses along flowering spikes that may be 1–2 feet in length. The foliage is medium to dark green, though new leaves sometimes have a definite bronze cast, particularly the red-blooming species.

How to Grow

Astilbes are hardy from zones 4–9. They prefer shady conditions and very deep, rich soil. Even moisture is beneficial to these plants, as they dry out easily, causing the plant to die. Where summers are hot and sweltering and winters are harsh, mulch with several inches of compost or bark chips. Remove the mulch in spring when new shoots first appear.

Flowering occurs in early summer to midsummer.

✎ Bernheim Arboretum and Research Forest

Although trees take center stage at Kentucky's Bernheim Arboretum, the plants growing at their feet add a touch of elegance to the forest. Many different kinds of hostas are found growing here, providing visitors with beautiful visual displays and a chance to see which of these species do well in their region.

Hosta (*Hosta* spp.)
Hostas have long been popular with gardeners, but the number of varieties available to the public has increased dramatically only over the last 20 years. The foliage is the real drawing card of these shade-loving plants, and today varieties are available with large leaves or small, dark green or with a bluish cast, edged or striped with white, yellow, or gold.

The lily-like blossom is not to be ignored, however, for spires of flowers of many species greatly enhance the beauty of the plant.

Gardeners can choose from over 400 hybrids, cultivars, and species. Although some of these only vary slightly from one another, others are quite distinct.

How to Grow
Hostas are tough, easy-to-grow, shade-loving plants, an almost unmatched blessing for many gardeners. They prefer rich soil with even moisture and light shade. Although in some gardens in the North and Midwest these plants can withstand direct sun, southern gardeners need to provide plenty of protection from the burning rays of the sun, particularly for those varieties with light-colored edges or stripes.

Established plants can be divided every few years to produce new plants. Dividing should be done in early spring when new growth begins to emerge. Replant divisions immediately. Fertilize with well-rotted manure during the active growing season. Although hostas are hardy, they are susceptible to damage from slugs and black vine weevils.

Kentucky

✎ Cave Hill and Lexington Cemeteries

Both Cave Hill and Lexington cemeteries have beautiful displays of trees and shrubs. Among the most beautiful of the trees grown at both cemeteries is the ginkgo, an ancient species that dates back from the time of the dinosaurs.

Ginkgoes are considered the oldest cultivated tree on earth. Sometimes called living fossils, they are extinct in the wild and are found growing only in cultivation.

Ginkgo *(Ginkgo biloba)*
The most distinguishing feature of the ginkgo tree is its small, fan-shaped leaf. The leaves resemble a frond of the maidenhair fern, and thus the tree is sometimes called the maidenhair tree. At maturity the ginkgo grows to be 125 feet tall. In autumn the leaves turn a soft yellow and then fall all at once.

This plant is dioeceous, meaning that it bears male and female flowers on different trees. Both kinds of flowers lack sepals and petals. Because the female trees bear a putrid fruit with a decidedly unpleasant odor, only male trees should be planted.

Young trees display a rather sprawling growth habit, but as they mature, the trees appear more graceful. Sometimes woody protrusions, looking like misplaced roots, appear along the branches and trunk. Called "Chi Chi" by the Japanese, these are considered signs of good luck.

How to Grow
Ginkgoes need full sun but are tolerant of a wide variety of environmental conditions. These trees are particularly useful in urban areas because they seem unaffected by air pollution. Ginkgoes are not usually bothered by pests and will grow in poor, compacted soils.

Prune young trees during dormant period to control unwanted branches.

✎ Shaker Village of Pleasant Hill and New Harmony

Early American herb gardens almost always included sweet-scented plants. Lavender is an herb native to Mediterranean regions and much loved throughout Europe; it is often associated with Old World countries such as England and France. Early pioneers brought lavender with them to the New World, and settlers at New Harmony and Shaker Village of Pleasant Hill grew it in their gardens. The

Shakers used lavender not for its beautiful spikes of purple flowers but for the oil extracted from the plant.

English Lavender *(Lavandula angustifolia)*

Lavender is a multibranched shrub bearing spikes of small purple flowers in June and July. It grows to a height of about 36 inches. The leaves are light green, somewhat hairy, and aromatic. Lavender shrubs can grow as much as 5 feet across.

English lavender is sometimes called *L. officinalis* or *L. delphinensis,* but is more often referred to as *L. angustifolia.* The fragrance of English lavender is deeper and richer than that of Spanish lavender, *L. latifolia,* which is often grown commercially.

Lavender blossoms can be dried to use in making potpourris or sachets. The oil from the flowers is used in herbal baths because it invigorates and cleanses the skin.

How to Grow

Lavender is hardy in zones 5–8 and prefers a slightly alkaline soil. For best growth, the soil should be sandy and well drained and the plants should be placed in full sun. Seeds are slow to germinate, so propagation is best done by taking stem cuttings in late summer. Protect from the cold where winter temperatures are severe.

lavender

Michigan

❧ Dow Gardens

Close to the herb display at Dow Gardens is a beautiful collection of hybrid lilies, considered by many to be the aristocrats of the summer garden. Popular garden plants for many centuries, lilies have long been a symbol of purity and innocence. During the Middle Ages, artists frequently painted female saints holding stalks of lilies.

In the garden, these plants produce exquisite flowers on top of long, slender stalks. Many of the 200 species that make up the genus Lilium are native to the United States and are among the most beautiful wildflowers. Oriental lilies, hybridized to create unusual shades and color combinations, may be even more lovely. Although there are no blue lilies, almost every other color is represented: white, cream, all shades of yellow and gold, pink, purple, and red.

Asiatic Lilies *(Lilium* spp.)

Given the right spot in the garden, lilies can be as durable and reliable as daffodils or crocuses, and most lilies will grow in every horticultural zone.

Lily flowers are large and deliciously colored and usually occur many to a stem. Lilies range in height from 2–6 feet. Flower forms include trumpet shape, pendant, flat-faced, and bowl-shaped.

How to Grow

It is important to spend time and effort preparing the bed. A little care and energy spent at the outset will reward you for years to come. Well-drained soil is crucial: If water stands on the bulbs, they will rot quickly. For best results, the soil should be slightly acid, full of organic matter, and well dug. During planting, add a bit of bone meal.

Most lilies can be planted in fall. Water the flowers well while in bloom and treat the plants to an all-purpose fertilizer as the stems emerge in spring.

A word of warning: deer find fresh, young lily stalks an irresistible delicacy.

❧ Cranbrook House and Gardens

Spring and summer bring incomparable colors to the flower borders at Cranbrook Gardens. Blossoms from bulbs, both common and unusual, blend with annuals and perennials to fill the planting beds. Among the most beautiful and unusual of these bulbs are the ornamental onions.

The onion, or Allium, family is composed of more than 500 species of both ornamental and culinary value. The family includes onion, garlic, leeks, and chives as well as many perennials grown simply for their beauty.

Giant Onion *(Allium giganteum)*

A very tall plant, giant onion usually reaches a height of 3–5 feet. The flower head is a perfect ball, 2–4 inches in diameter, made up of over 100 tiny purple star-shaped flowers. It usually takes several weeks for the plant to bloom after the flower stalk first appears in early summer.

Leaves are 5–8 inches wide and form a basal rosette. Unlike the leaves of other bulbs, the foliage of allium dies back almost as soon as the flowers quit blooming. Giant onion should be planted in groups of three or more. Other allium species of ornamental value include Persian onion, blue globe onion, and star of Persia.

How to Grow

Plant alliums in the fall in any good garden soil where they receive full sun. Planting depth should be approximately 2–3 times the diameter of the bulb. Bulbs should be spaced 6–18 inches apart, depending on the mature height of the plant. Alliums can be used as cut flowers, although their oniony odor is often a bit disagreeable. To eliminate this odor, soak the freshly cut stems in a container of water for several minutes, then place in a vase with new water.

❦ MICHIGAN STATE UNIVERSITY HORTICULTURAL DEMONSTRATION GARDENS

Flowers appear in huge numbers at the Demonstration Gardens on this university campus, and among the most colorful are the petunias. Every summer this garden grows over one hundred new petunia cultivars in conjunction with the All America Selection testing.

Petunia (*Petunia* spp.)

Petunias have not always been so colorful, nor so beloved. Spanish explorers first found this small plant growing near the coast of Argentina, and although it displayed a few white flowers, it was not particularly pretty. In 1831 a different species of petunia was found growing in Argentina; plant breeders hybridized the two, and the results were stunning. New plants came in bright, beautiful colors, and petunias quickly became extraordinarily popular.

Petunias are divided into two classes, grandiflora and multiflora. Grandifloras have large blossoms and include cultivars such as 'Purple Pirouette', which has reddish-purple blossoms edged in white. Each blossom measures 3½–4 inches across. 'Cascade' has even larger blossoms, sometimes measuring 4½ inches across. Multifloras such as 'Comanche' have smaller blossoms but more of them.

How to Grow

Petunias love hot, dry weather. New cultivars have been developed to extend the blooming season and make the plants more tolerant to variations in weather.

Set petunia plants out in spring after all danger of frost has passed. Place them where they will receive full sun in soils that are light and well drained. Dry, sandy soil is best. If your soil has a high clay content, choose single varieties over doubles for best results.

❦ 4-H CHILDREN'S GARDEN

One of the favorite spots in the Children's Garden on the campus of Michigan State University is the Pizza Garden, where children and grownups can see "pizza in the raw," a collection of plants whose products often top one of America's favorite foods.

The round garden is divided into wedge-shaped "slices," each piece containing a different plant. Although most of the plants are authentic to the making of a pizza, cheese is represented by bright orange-yellow marigolds.

Tomato

Any tomato plant will do, but it's more fun to plant "kid-sized" tomatoes such as the Roma VF variety, which bears small fruit with thick flesh—perfect for making pizza sauce. Tomatoes need full sun and rich soil.

Oregano

There are many different kinds of oreganoes, but Greek Oregano is the one to plant because the flavor is superior to that of other varieties. Oregano grown from seed has tremendous variation in its flavor, so it's better to find a small nursery-grown plant, sniff the leaves to make sure it smells pungent, and use this. Flavorful oreganoes seem to have white flowers.

Basil

Another essential herb for a pizza, basil is used in many Italian recipes. The leaves smell like licorice. While this plant withstands heat well, it is very tender and the first hint of frost turns it black. Plant from seed or plant small nursery-grown plants after all danger of frost has passed. It needs full sun and even moisture. Space 10 inches apart.

Onions

White, red, or yellow onion sets can be planted. These can be harvested while the tops are still green, at which point they are known as 'scallions.' Needs full sun, ordinary to rich soil.

Parsley

The best-tasting parsley is flat-leaf. This is a biennial plant most often grown as an annual. Seeds are very slow to germinate, so be sure to treat them first by soaking in hot water, or by placing in the refrigerator or freezer. Parsley will withstand light shade but does best in full sun. It prefers moist conditions.

❦ W. J. BEAL BOTANICAL GARDEN

The sunflower is a native American plant, beloved by pioneers, worshiped by the Incas. Not only is it a beautiful ornamental, it is also much prized by industries which extract the oil for cooking, canning, and making paint pigments. Native Americans had many uses for the plant. They would grind the seeds into meal and flower and use fibers from the stalks to make cloth.

The sunflower is one of the few plants originating in the continental United States that is considered economically important worldwide.

Sunflower *(Helianthus annuus)*

Sunflowers can grow to be impressively tall—over 8 feet in some cases. The triangular leaves are 3–12 inches long and the stunning, bright yellow blossoms, which come in late summer, are sometimes as much as 12 inches across.

How to Grow

Sunflowers are prairie or field plants and consequently need hours of full sun daily. They tolerate a wide variety of soils but should be planted in a well-drained area.

Although the common sunflower is perhaps best known and most widely recognized, it is not necessarily the best species to grow in home gardens. For a slightly shorter plant that blends more readily into the landscape, try *Helianthus angustifolius,* Swamp Sunflower, hardy in zones 6–9. With sufficient sun this will grow to be a sturdy 5- to 6-foot plant covered with small sunflower blossoms in fall. In shade, the plants can grow to 10 feet or more, but they will be spindly with fewer blooms.

Minnesota

✄ Minnesota Landscape Arboretum

The prairie at the Minnesota Landscape Arboretum is a place of beauty. Tall grasses wave gently in the breeze, parting long enough for colorful wildflowers to appear like jewels in a sea of green.

The dominant wildflower species found in the prairie belong either to the legume or the composite family, the latter being composed of dozens of familiar plants such as coneflower, sunflower, black-eyed Susan, and coreopsis.

These prairie plants are generally easy to grow and require little maintenance. Many are valuable both in a formal and a naturalized landscape.

Coreopsis *(Coreopsis lanceolata)*

This perennial wildflower has bright yellow blossoms 2–2½ inches across. It likes well-aerated soil that is not too rich, and it performs well in full sun or light shade. Plants can be divided in fall or spring, and divisions should be replanted immediately and given extra moisture until the plants are well established. Coreopsis also grows easily from seed and will bloom the second year. Seeds need light to germinate, so sow them on the surface and keep them moist.

coreopsis

Black-eyed Susan *(Rudbeckia hirta)*

This short-lived perennial is well known throughout the United States. In some areas this wildflower may become invasive and difficult to control. Close watch should be kept on this prolific plant when it is introduced into a formal garden because it can easily outgrow its welcome.

Black-eyed Susan grows to a height of 24–36 inches and has yellow flowers with a dark brown or black center. A highly adaptable plant, Black-eyed Susan will withstand heavy or light, rich or sterile soils, regular watering or drought conditions. It grows very easily from seed.

Prairie Coneflower *(Ratibida columnaris)*

Native from southwestern Canada to northern Mexico, it grows 36 inches tall and has yellow or yellow-and-red blossoms. Native Americans extracted a dye from the blossoms and made tea from the leaves and flower heads. This plant needs full sun and dry, well-drained soils. Seeds may be sown in fall or spring and should germinate within 5 to 10 days, blooming the second growing season.

✄ Noerenberg Gardens

The small, lush gardens at Noerenberg Gardens on Lake Minnetonka hold many beautiful, cultivated flowers, but perhaps none are more lovely than the native penstemons.

The genus *Penstemon* includes hundreds of different species, both annuals and perennials. There is as much variation in their environmental needs as there is in their appearance. Some like very wet conditions, while other species need it quite dry. Each individual species is particular about where it grows, however, making it tricky to cultivate them outside their native range. These plants do best in the West and Midwest where wet winter soils are generally not a problem.

Penstemon *(Penstemon* spp.)

Although many garden penstemons are actually perennials, some are treated as annuals because they are not reliably hardy. Penstemons vary in size from 2 inches to 6 feet and are useful for filling different landscape needs. Short, shrubby types work well in the rock garden; taller varieties look good in planting beds or mixed borders.

Some of the best species to include in the garden are: Scarlet bugler *(P. barbatus).* This penstemon grows 2–6 feet tall and puts forth flowering stems of pink, purple, or red in summer. Cultivars include 'Bashful', with orange flowers on 12- to 14-inch plants; 'Crystal', with white flowers; and 'Prairie Dawn', with pale pink flowers.

P. cardinalis has rich, deep red blossoms borne on 3-foot stems in summer. Foxglove beard-tongue *(P. digitalis)* produces white flowers that look like those of foxglove.

How to Grow

The greatest demand of penstemons is for well-drained soil; this plant will not tolerate wet roots. Cold hardiness varies from one species to another, as does tolerance to high temperatures. Light exposure should be full sun to partial shade and soils should be neutral (with pH around 7). Plant in early spring and space 1–3 feet apart. Penstemons can be propagated by seed, or by tip and stem cuttings.

Missouri

✎ Missouri Botanical Garden

Most Japanese gardens contain plants that are both pleasing to the eye and rich in symbolism. The Japanese garden at the Missouri Botanical Garden is no exception. The majority of the plants found in this garden are evergreen and represent many different kinds of dwarf conifers, including pines. The pine is a symbol of longevity and long life.

Mugo Pine *(Pinus mugo mugo)*

The genus *Pinus* includes species which grow from 2 feet to 100 feet tall. Dwarf pines such as Swiss mountain pine *(P. mugo)* or Mugo pine *(P. mugo mugo)* are both used often in dwarf conifer collections or as focal points in a Japanese garden. These are low, mounding shrubs, generally wider than they are tall. The cultivar 'Compacta' has dark green needles; it grows only 4 feet tall and spreads to about 6 feet across. 'Pumilo' is slightly smaller, growing 2 feet tall and 4 feet across.

The Japanese stone pine *(P. pumila)* produces needles 1–3 inches long and reaches a height of 2 feet.

How to Grow

While most pines need full sun, some of the dwarf varieties, such as Swiss mountain pine, will also thrive in partial shade. If they are grown in well-drained soil, these small shrubs need no maintenance other than weeding and annual pruning. Fallen needles provide a natural mulch and they are seldom troubled either by pests or disease.

Many pine species can also be trained as bonsai. The best species to use for this are Swiss mountain pine, Japanese white pine, Japanese black pine, and Scots pine.

Ohio

✎ Cleveland Botanical Garden

An herb garden contains plants that are useful in any number of ways. Most herb gardens will display herbs used for cooking and flavoring, for medicines, for perfume, and for crafts such as dyeing fibers.

The Cleveland Botanical Garden has a garden set aside primarily for the display of dye plants. From these plants it is possible to obtain nearly every color in the rainbow, from black and blue to gold, pinks, and purples.

When dyeing fibers it is necessary to use chemicals—such as tin, alum, and chrome—called mordants. These "lock in" the pigments and prevent them from fading. Different chemicals used with the same plants will produce different colors.

The following is a list of easy to grow dye plants and the mordants used to produce various colors.

Barberry (inner bark)	none	yellow
(all parts)	Iron	dark green
Bloodroot (roots)	none	orange
(roots)	Alum	rust
Dock (young leaves)	Chrome	red
Elderberry (berries)	Alum	violet
(berries)	Chrome	blue
Feverfew (leaves, stems)	Chrome	greenish-yellow
Marigold (flowers)	Chrome	gold
Onion (yellow skins)	Alum	burnt orange
(yellow skins)	Iron	brown
Potentilla (roots)	Chrome	brown-red
(roots)	Iron	purple-red
Rosemary (leaves, flowers)	Alum	yellow-green
St.-John's wort (tops)	Alum	yellow-buff

✎ The Dawes Arboretum

The tree collections at The Dawes Arboretum include both rare and common species. One of the most beautiful, yet ordinary, of these is the river birch, whose bark—which peels and curls as it ages—has had many different uses, including kindling, paper, insulation, and as material to make plates, baskets, and canoes. Native Americans dipped sticks in vegetable inks to write on the bark, using for the most part a pictorial language. Images of paddlers in a birch-bark canoe have been firmly planted in our imaginations for many years, thanks to Henry Wadsworth Longfellow's poem, "The Song of Hiawatha," which begins "Give me of your bark, O Birch-tree."

River Birch *(Betula nigra)*

This tree grows 60–80 feet tall and has distinctive reddish-brown, curling bark. The oval leaves measure 1½–3½ inches long. In spring, catkins (drooping stalks of flowers) appear and are followed by small conelike fruit in fall.

There are approximately 50 to 60 different species of birches, most of which are native to North America and Asia. In general, birch bark varies in color from one species to another from white to silver, yellow to reddish-brown, and sometimes almost black.

How to Grow

River birch is tolerant of a wide variety of environmental conditions and can withstand moist or even wet soils. This species grows naturally from Massachusetts to Florida westward and is hardy in horticultural zones 5–10. It is resistant to the bronze birch borer, which proves to be a serious problem in many other species.

Birches generally prefer full sun and do not like to be transplanted. They are best planted in early spring.

❧ FELLOWS RIVERSIDE GARDENS

One of the most beautiful of all landscaping trends during the past few years is the recognition and inclusion of beautiful vegetables in the flower garden. Edible landscaping has long been popular, but Fellows Riverside Gardens has taken this a step further and has included hundreds of attractive herbs and vegetables, such as parsley and red-stemmed Swiss chard, among the traditional plantings of begonias, petunias, and marigolds. Although parsley has been used as a garnish on a plate since Roman times, it is now also being used as a garnish in the garden.

Parsley *(Petroselinum crispum)*

Many different kinds of parsley are available to the home gardener, meeting many different needs. For the cook, flat-leaf parsley has superior flavor and is excellent for flavoring a variety of dishes.

Perhaps the most beautiful parsley, often used as garnish, is curly-leaf parsley. It forms an attractive, compact plant with bright green ruffled leaves.

How to Grow

Parsley can be grown easily from seed, although germination sometimes takes up to 6 weeks. Superstition holds that parsley is so slow to germinate because it goes to the devil 9 times before coming out above ground. To speed germination, seeds can be treated by soaking, refrigerating, or freezing.

Parsley is a biennial that is generally grown as an annual.

The second year the plant will bolt and go to seed and is not as attractive as first-year plants. Parsley is hardy to zone 9; it prefers moderately rich, well-drained soil and full sun to partial shade.

To maintain parsley as an ornamental plant, keep it carefully weeded and cut back any flowering stalks.

❧ INNISWOOD METRO GARDENS

The herb garden at Inniswood Metro Gardens is well known for its collection of thymes. The genus *Thymus* includes plants that trail or climb, are used as a shrub or a ground cover, and produce lavender, pink, or white flowers. Thyme is used as an ornamental plant in the garden, as flavoring in cooking, and as a treatment for various ailments, including asthma, whooping cough, and stomach cramps.

Thyme *(Thymus* spp.)

Many different species of thyme grow well in gardens throughout the United States. Some of the best species and cultivars include:

Lemon thyme *(T. × citriodorus)* is a small shrub 4–12 inches high, with dark green, glossy leaves bearing a strong lemon scent. The cultivar 'Argenteus' is called silver thyme for the white edging around each leaf. Silver thyme has a trailing habit and is good to use cascading over a rock wall or in a hanging basket.

Common thyme *(T. vulgaris)* has oval, gray-green leaves and tiny white or purplish flowers. It grows 6–15 inches in height. Mother-of-thyme *(T. praecox arcticus)* only grows to 4 inches tall. It has dark green leaves and is used as a thick, aromatic ground cover.

How to Grow

Thyme needs light, well-drained soil, and full sun or partial shade. Most species are hardy in zones 5–9. Propagate by division in early spring.

❧ KINGWOOD CENTER

The peony collection at Kingwood Center announces the arrival of spring in the most glorious fashion imaginable. Big round blossoms of white, red, and pink make winter blues a thing of the distant past.

Peonies have been beloved for many centuries. In China, the peony is a symbol of prosperity. The plant was named for Paeon, physician to the Greek gods. Probably because of the influence of this legend, peonies were used for hundreds of years to cure aches and pains. Peony tea was given to pregnant women to ease the pain of childbirth.

Peony (*Paeonia* spp.)

Peony blossoms are large, some measuring over 6 inches across. The flowers are borne on semi-woody shrubby plants growing to a height of 32–36 inches.

How to Grow

Peonies are long-lived plants; some have reportedly lasted over 100 years. They tolerate a wide range of soils, but will bloom best in neutral or slightly alkaline soils that are light, fertile, and rich in organic matter. Because planting depth is crucial to their growth and development, it is safest to prepare the planting hole about two weeks ahead of time and allow the soil to settle.

Plant divisions or nursery-grown plants in fall so that the eyes on the roots are 1½ inches below soil level. If the roots are set too deep, the plants will not bloom.

Peonies need good sun and plenty of moisture. During the growing season, treat them to several layers of organic mulch.

✂ Kingwood Center (extra)

Wildflowers are often brought into a formal garden with wonderful success. This is true of the small pink evening primrose, native to the south-central United States. Forming a carpet of pink, with a backing of dark green, finely cut foliage, this small wildflower blends beautifully with perennials and annuals of late spring and early summer found at Kingwood Center.

Showy Evening Primrose (*Oenothera speciosa*)

In spite of the common name, this species opens during the daylight hours. The flowers are 1–2 inches in length, the leaves 1–3 inches long. Overall height of the plant is 12–24 inches. Each blossom has four rounded petals, which are white when they first come out, then turn pink and finally rose. Center stamens are golden-yellow. This species looks best when planted in masses.

How to Grow

If grown in moderately rich soil and full sun, the plant is compact and attractive. If too rich a soil is supplied, or there is not enough sun, the plants tend to get lanky and the foliage outshines the flowers. Evening primrose grows easily from seeds, which can be pur-chased through wild-flower seed-company catalogs. Sow seeds outdoors as soon as the soil can be worked. Germination is slow, sometimes taking as long as 25 days.

A word of caution: Like many other species in this genus, showy evening primrose does not always know when to quit and sometimes becomes slightly invasive. Keep a careful eye on it to make sure it stays within bounds.

✂ Stan Hywet Hall and Gardens

The estate garden of Stan Hywet offers the visitor glimpses of old-fashioned flowers, grown when the Seiberlings lived in the house, as well as beautiful new cultivars which they would have loved to have included, had they been available.

One of the most exciting new twists to an old plant is the double impatiens, which looks almost like a miniature rose. Double impatiens come in full double and semi-double forms and are usually pink or red.

In the Seiberlings' day, impatiens were known as busy lizzies. The name impatiens was supposedly given to this plant because the seed pods explode when ripe, shooting seeds a long distance from the plants.

Impatiens (*I. wallerana*)

Different varieties and cultivars of impatiens come in a wide array of colors including red, pink, white, salmon, violet, and a recently released yellow hybrid. The largest-flowering hybrids have a blossom that measures 2½ inches across. Double varieties are generally much smaller and only measure 1¼ inches in diameter.

How to Grow

Impatiens do not like excessively dry conditions and are completely intolerant of frost. For best results, plant seeds indoors 10–14 weeks before the last frost.

These plants tolerate high heat if sufficient moisture is available. Wilting during hot summer days does not necessarily indicate a need for water, but may be caused by heat stress. If wilting and yellow leaves occur, increase watering.

Impatiens are known as shade plants but they must have at least some sunlight to bloom well. They can be grown in full sun if sufficient moisture is supplied.

✂ The Morton Arboretum

Late spring at The Morton Arboretum means rhododendrons in full bloom, and the Rhododendron Garden becomes the most popular place at the arboretum.

Rhododendrons are evergreen shrubs with showy flowers. Many people are easily confused by rhododendron nomenclature. All azaleas belong to the rhododendron family, but few are commonly called "rhododendrons." The difference between plants commonly called "azalea" and those called "rhododendron" include the following points: Azaleas have small, narrow, pointed leaves, slightly

peony

hairy along the midrib, and flowers borne along the margins and the tips of the branches. The plants commonly called rhododendrons have much broader leaves that occur in whorls; their flowers are generally single and borne in clusters at the ends of the branches.

Rhododendron (*Rhododendron* spp.)

Different rhododendron species display different tolerances to extreme temperatures, some being quite sensitive to cold weather, others withstanding frigid temperatures with apparently few bad effects.

Rhododendrons are available both as species that occur in the wild and as cultivars or hybrids bred for a particular color, size of blossom, or hardiness. To find the best rhododendrons for your own region, determine which are native to your area, and which hybrids or cultivars are grown successfully at the closest display garden.

How to Grow

Both rhododendrons and azaleas like partial shade and rich, acid soils. If necessary, add generous amounts of organic matter before planting. The roots of these plants are generally found close to the soil surface and should be mulched to protect them from temperature fluctuations.

Rhododendrons should be fed lightly when buds appear in spring. After flowering, prune carefully, only down to the next whorl of leaves.

Wisconsin

✂ Boerner Botanical Gardens

Each June the Friends of Boerner Botanical Gardens host a rose festival that draws rose lovers from far and near. The rose is America's favorite flower, people flock to the festival to attend the seminars and lectures and to view the thousands of sweet-scented beautiful blossoms that are planted in the Botanical Garden in late spring and early summer.

Roses are the oldest of all cultivated flowers. During Medieval times, roses were grown primarily for food and medicine, and not for their beauty.

Roses are dedicated to the god of silence, Harpocrates; even today, the term sub rosa means confidential, or in secret.

Rose (*Rosa* spp.)

Roses show tremendous variation, from miniatures that grow only 6–8 inches tall to very large ramblers and shrubs. Their environmental needs, particularly tolerance to cold, also vary. Some roses only tolerate temperatures to 20°F, while others will withstand temperatures as low as −20°F.

In general, roses should be planted in deep, rich, slightly acid soil that drains well. For best blooms, plant in full sun.

Place mulch, such as pine nuggets or pine straw, around the plants in early summer to discourage weeds and retain moisture.

Most roses should be pruned in late winter or early spring. Use sharp, clean clippers and cut diagonally across the stem.

Feeding will depend on the type of rose grown; old-fashioned types need less fertilizer than the newer hybrid teas. Although many rose varieties have been bred for resistance to disease, many are still susceptible to problems from black spot and mildew. In addition, a number of insect pests, including Japanese beetles, thrips, leaf rollers, aphids, and spider mites, also find roses to be quite tasty. An insecticidal soap or hand picking may be enough to take care of these unwanted pests. If chemical controls are necessary, check with a local county extension agent or a nearby botanical garden.

✂ Mitchell Park Conservatory

The orchid collection at the Mitchell Park Conservatory is one of the most beautiful of all the displays. These tropical flowers are loved throughout the world for their intricately patterned blossoms. Although orchids are exacting in their environmental needs, it is possible to grow them in a sunny window in your own home, if they are given the right light, temperature, and humidity.

Cattleya Orchid (*Cattleya* spp.)

These orchids grow 24–26 inches tall and have large, scented flowers 4–8 inches across, 2–6 to a stem. Flowers appear any time between September and June and last from 10–25 days.

Cattleyas need indirect sunlight (or light from fluorescent tubes), good air circulation, watering, mild feeding, and frequent misting. These orchids can be grown outdoors during summer months, if they are provided with protection from direct sun.

If using fluorescent bulbs, place them 6 inches from the top of the plant for 10–12 hours daily. To help keep humidity high, put the plants in trays filled with gravel and water, and mist them frequently. Allow the soil to dry out before watering. On sunny days be sure to water early in the day to keep water spots from forming on the leaves.

Most orchids thrive on warmth and relative humidity of 65%–70%. Cattleyas are considered intermediate in their temperature requirements and will do best when night

rhododendron

temperatures range from 58°–60°F with daytime temperatures 10°–15°F higher.

Cattleyas, like almost all orchids, need a dormant period. While they are dormant, water only enough to keep the plants alive. During the active growing season, feed plants with a liquid orchid fertilizer every other week.

❧ OLD WORLD WISCONSIN

Many heirloom vegetables grow in the pioneer gardens at Old World Wisconsin. Because we are accustomed to the picture-perfect vegetable varieties that we grow in our own gardens or buy at the market, some of these old-fashioned vegetables look a bit misshapen and insignificant. But their beauty may lie in outstanding flavor or good resistance to disease rather than symmetry and color. Nowadays old-fashioned gardeners, gardening historians, and people who simply remember grandma's vegetables as being the best are helping heirloom flowers and vegetables stage a comeback.

Newer strains, admittedly, produce larger fruits and vegetables, but is bigger necessarily better? Older varieties often display characteristics that make them highly desirable for home gardeners. Some are easier to grow and harvest in small gardens than many of the new cultivars available today. Others simply taste better to some people, even if memory is influenced by romantic notions of grandma's garden.

Many people today assume that a century ago, gardeners only had a few varieties to choose from. This is not so. For example, in 1900, catalogs listed over 200 varieties of beans. Unfortunately, many of the varieties available to grandma are no longer in existence. Less than 20 percent of the turn-of-the-century bean varieties are still available through the nursery trade today.

Heirloom vegetables are nonhybrid, meaning that selective breeding has been done to choose seeds of plants that display various characteristics, such as size, color, or tolerance to cold temperatures, but these have not been cross-bred with other plants.

Gardeners who wish to grow heirloom vegetables must keep each line separate, because if the vegetables are to stay true to the parent plant, they must not be allowed to cross-breed. The separation can be either time or space. Different varieties can be planted on a schedule so that they bloom at different times, or they can be planted far enough apart so that pollen will not be exchanged.

Finding heirloom plants can be both challenging and fun. Some are available through programs such as the non-profit Seed Saver's Exchange, where members save and swap seeds from older vegetable varieties. Other seeds can be found during afternoon excursions to the country, where a simple flower or vegetable might catch your eye. Pay particular attention to abandoned homesites—you might find some real treasures.

Heirloom seeds hold magical combinations of genes that make each unique. It's difficult to predict what horticultural needs we will have in the years to come, and the particular genetic combinations which make up the flowers and vegetables of earlier days may prove to be important to us in the future.

❧ THE PAINE ART CENTER AND ARBORETUM

The beautiful flower borders at The Paine Art Center and Arboretum are enhanced by the color and fragrance of many different species. Among the most attractive of these are various members of the genus *Salvia*.

Salvia (*Salvia* spp.)

Because salvia displays such diversity, members of this genus can be used well in both formal and naturalized gardens. Salvias can be both annuals and perennials, mounding bedding plants as well as multibranched shrubs. The genus *Salvia* also includes the culinary herb sage, which is used extensively in cooking and flavoring.

Perhaps the best known flowering sage is the popular bedding plant *Salvia splendens,* which shows brilliant spires of bright red blossoms. Recent cultivars have been introduced in many colors, including white, pink, and deep purple, although red remains by far the most popular color.

Perennial sage *(S. farinacea)* is sometimes called mealy-cup sage. It comes in delicate colors of blue and white, shades that have given rise to cultivar names such as 'Victoria' and 'Porcelain White.'

How to Grow

Salvias are considered easy to grow and tolerate a wide range of environmental conditions. They will grow in any good garden soil with a pH of around 7, need full sun, and prefer evenly moist soil.

In very hot regions, the plant can be planted in partial shade where they receive some protection from the sun. These plants are readily available at local nurseries and garden centers. Well established perennial plants can be divided in fall or early spring. For bushy plants, pinch back seedlings until early summer.

Tips for Photographing Flowers

Allen Rokach and Anne Millman

Look at flowers from all directions, become aware of the background, and check the edges of frame to include only what is important to the image.

Equipment

🌿 A 35mm camera is preferred, because it is portable, adaptable, and includes a "through the lens" viewfinder.

🌿 A 55mm macro lens is ideal for close-ups; screw-on magnifying lenses (+1, +2, +4 diopters) are less expensive alternatives.

🌿 A tripod is a must for flower photography to maintain sharpness with slow shutter speeds. Using a tripod allows the photographer to concentrate on composition and technical matters.

🌿 Several filters are recommended. A polarizing filter removes unwanted reflections and glare, and helps deepen the blue of the sky. A 1A skylight filter protects the lens. A soft-focus filter helps create a romantic effect. An 81A or B filter "warms up" a flower.

🌿 An electronic flash is invaluable for stopping motion, getting extreme sharpness, and maximizing depth of field.

Light

🌿 Analyze light in terms of intensity, direction, and color. The creative use of available light can transform the ordinary into the extraordinary. For a translucent effect light must pass through a flower from behind. Sidelight brings out texture, line, and form. Early morning and late afternoon light bathe a scene in a wash of color. Misty light after a rain saturates and enriches colors.

🌿 Develop patience, to cope with changing light conditions and movements. Don't just wait but analyze, anticipate, and be ready to shoot when conditions are right.

Exposure

🌿 For greater accuracy, take a meter reading within 6 inches of the flower and lock in that reading before composing the shot.

🌿 Proper exposure is always tricky, so bracket it to ensure good results.

🌿 Start with a shot at the meter reading; then overexpose and underexpose by one full f/stop. Underexposure deepens colors and darkens backgrounds, while overexposure produces pastels.

Sharpness

🌿 Focus on the pictorial element that must be sharp, even if other parts of the flower or scene will not be perfectly sharp. A flower shot against a dark shadow in the background appears sharper because of its well-defined edge.

🌿 To increase the area of sharpness—called depth of field—use the highest f/stop (smallest aperture). Adding light, with a reflector or flash, makes it possible to use a higher f/stop.

Flowers can be enchantingly rendered with blurs or an "out-of-focus" effect. Well-planned blurs can be produced using selective focus, by letting movement register at a slow shutter speed, or by deliberately moving the camera during a long exposure.

Composition

Fill the frame with the flower, or shoot only sections of a flower. Don't include the background unless it adds to the final image.

Look for lines and shapes to help structure your composition. Strong diagonals, such as paths in a garden, create a sense of depth. Curves and radial patterns add visual interest.

Apply the "rule of thirds" for organizing horizontal or vertical bands within the composition.

Composing pictures indoors at flower shows and conservatories provides several advantages, as there are no wind or erratic movements of a flower and the lighting is uniform.

Create images with flowers, not just images of flowers. Use form, color, texture, and pattern as a basis for composition.

General Suggestions

Define the purpose of your photograph. Ask yourself, "Why am I taking this picture? What am I trying to convey?" Your answer should be very specific, e.g., "This photograph is designed to convey the flower's unique shape."

Make a simple statement by practicing visual restraint. Eliminate whatever is extraneous.

Look at flowers from new and different perspectives. Peek inside, look from the rear, and don't neglect flowers past their prime.

Focus carefully and with purpose. In close-ups, the entire picture cannot always be sharp, so be sure that the essential pictorial element is perfectly sharp.

To get the shot you envision, be prepared to go to such lengths as lying on the ground, wading in water, or getting up before dawn.

Acknowledgments

Allen Rokach

I am grateful to Susan Costello, a terrific editor, who offered me the opportunity to take the photographs for this important book project.

Thanks to many new friends in the botanical community who smoothed the way so that the images were easier to take, especially Meegan McCarthy Bilow of the Chicago Botanic Garden; Carl Suk of the Bernheim Arboretum and Research Forest in Kentucky; Judith A. Gause of The Holden Arboretum in Ohio; James W. Sutherland of Cantigny in Illinois; Karen A. Petroff of the Mill Creek Park (Fellows Riverside Gardens) in Youngstown, Ohio; William J. Radler of Boerner Botanical Gardens in Milwaukee; Leroy F. Squires of Cave Hill Cemetery in Louisville, Kentucky; Marchetta L. Sparrow of Shaker Village of Pleasant Hill in Kentucky; Tina Oliver of Cranbrook House and Gardens in Michigan; and Jim Nachel of The Morton Arboretum in Illinois.

Special thanks and some final words of appreciation to my friend Frank Kecko, a caring and helpful companion who made our picture-taking trips memorable.

Index

Photography Credits